TRIED & TRUE

Eleven Principles of Church Growth from Frazer Memorial United Methodist Church

John Ed Mathison

DISCIPLESHIP RESOURCES

MATERIALS FOR GROWTH IN CHRISTIAN FAITH AND LIFE

P.O. Box 189 • Nashville. TN 37202 • Phone (615) 340-7284

Unless otherwise indicated, all scriptural quotations are taken from the New Revised Standard Version of the Holy Bible, copyright © 1989 by the Division of Christian Education of the National Council of Churches of Christ in the U.S.A. Used by permission.

ISBN 0-88177-117-1

Library of Congress Catalog Card Number: 92-71309

DR117

CONTENTS

PREFACE

Frazer Memorial Methodist Church began in 1889 when a local preacher organized a Sunday school in a storeroom on Holt Street in Montgomery, Alabama. The group started to grow and purchased a house on Heron Street as a meeting place. In 1892 a minister was assigned to the group and the church was organized. In 1898 property was purchased on Clayton Street and the name was changed to Clayton Street Methodist Church. The church remained there and grew. In 1937 the name of the church was changed from Clayton Street to Frazer Memorial.

In the 1960s Frazer Memorial Church had about 500 members. Interstates 85 and 65 were planned to intersect just a few blocks west of the church. This intersection required the purchase of large plots of land near the church building. Most people in the parish area had to relocate to other sections of the city. It became apparent that the interstate system had destroyed the neighborhood concept around which Frazer Memorial was built.

A committee was formed to discuss the future of Frazer Memorial. Most of the members had relocated to different parts of the city. Relocation of the church property would be difficult because there was no particular section of the city to which many members had moved. Some local consultants, and outside consultants from the denominational headquarters, were involved in the decision making. Because the members had relocated to such different geographical locations in the city, the consultants basically suggested that the church disband and encourage the members to join Methodist congregations near their new residences.

The committee at Frazer insisted that God still had a future for their congregation and that some means of relocation should be worked out. Initially some property in the south section of the city was offered to Frazer. The congregation actually purchased a parsonage near that property. However, some events led district leaders to give that property to another congregation. The consultants came back to the local committee at Frazer and again suggested that the church should probably disband.

At this point the pastor, Rev. Noah Lisenby, is reported to have leaped out of his chair about four feet into the air, looked at the people present, and said, "You may know statistics and demographics, but you don't know the heart of the people of Frazer, and you don't understand God's purpose for these people!" Noah Lisenby died just after that, but his dream and assessment of God's plan for Frazer became stronger every day. The people of Frazer felt that God had a plan and a purpose for them.

Eventually, five acres of property were offered to the church in East Montgomery. Again, the people of Frazer were told that relocation would not work because there was not a single member living within three miles of the new property! It was estimated that fewer than 50 percent of the people would relocate. Again, people did not know the heart of the Frazer family. At the time of relocation, Frazer did not lose a single member!

In 1970, about 400 people relocated to the eastern section of the city. In the last twenty years, Frazer has become one of the fastest growing United Methodist congregations in America. In 1990 it had the largest worship attendance and the largest Sunday school attendance of any United Methodist congregation in North America!

The planning model described here is one that Frazer Memorial began using when it had about 700 members. Today, with over 6,000 members, Frazer is still using this model. The model should be applicable to all sizes of congregations, because it is simply a vehicle into which information is fed and from which information will be developed to design new ministries. The model is something like a computer—the information placed into it will determine the strategies of ministry that emerge from it. The model can be used as effectively in a small congregation as in a large one, because strategies for ministry are firmly grounded in the facts of each situation.

If there are those who still doubt, who look at the title of this book and say, "What happened at Frazer Memorial could never happen in my congregation," let me share the following story. A few years ago a man who was an officer in the Air Force was serving as the chairman of Frazer's Evangelism Work Area. He was involved in developing and utilizing the model described in this book. He also had received a local preacher's license years before when he had considered the possibility of Christian ministry. A couple of small rural congregations were available at annual conference with no pastor to assign to those churches. The district superintendent approached me with the idea of appointing this man on a part-time basis to those rural congregations. Through our consultation together, the layman at Frazer was assigned as a part-time pastor to those congregations.

The layman was excited about the ministry for which he had been selected at Frazer. Now he was being invited to serve two rural congregations that had seen steady decline in recent years. He wanted to utilize the model he had helped develop at Frazer to see if it would be applicable in rural congregations which had not received any new members in recent years. It was a good opportunity to test this model in that situation.

After serving these congregations a few months and following the model that will be projected in this book, the layman called me one Saturday and wanted to know if it would be possible to borrow a robe because he was going to baptize three people the next day. I asked him to explain how this was happening and he said, "We are just utilizing the same model we used at Frazer, and we have three unchurched people who have been attending and want to join on profession of faith!" About one month later, he called again to say he was baptizing two families the next day. Both of these families were unchurched, had been invited by lay people, and wanted to become a part of the church.

All of a sudden, a small rural congregation that had received no members for several years was discovering that there were unchurched people in the area and that they would attend at the invitation of lay people from those local churches. Both of those small rural congregations began to receive members. This is an example of how this model can be used in congregations of different sizes.

In one sense, this is the story of Frazer Memorial United Methodist Church in Montgomery, Alabama. You will notice as you read that I (the author, John Ed Mathison) often refer to the members and groups of Frazer by name. I also sometimes speak in the first person pronoun ("I") when I refer to myself. This is not intended to exalt myself or the people at Frazer, but rather to speak directly to you from what has been tested in our own experience. For, you see, though this is the Frazer story in one sense, in another it is a story for all congregations.

More accurately, it contains a *model* of planning for church growth that can be applied in practically any congregation—rural, urban, small, medium, large, transitional, etc.

Please don't confuse the story, the illustrations from Frazer, with the model itself. In so doing you could miss the potential that the model holds for you in your setting. Adjust the illustrations as you need to, to fit the realities of your congregation—but take heart from the Frazer story: Your church can grow!

J. E. M.
Montgomery, Alabama
Spring 1992

CHAPTER 1
DESIGNATE a PLANNING GROUP

The first step toward developing a model for growth is to designate a planning group. At Frazer we call this group our "Joel Committee." The name "Joel" is taken from the Old Testament prophet who encouraged "the old men to dream dreams and the young men to see visions" (paraphrase of Joel 2:28*b*). Whatever you choose to call it, this is the group that will develop each of the other steps in your model for growth and ministry.

Prayerful Planning

Prayerful planning is essential for growth. Every congregation needs to have some group prayerfully planning for the future and open to God's plan for the congregation. The church is called into existence by God and God has a purpose and a plan for each congregation. It is part of the task of the church to discover God's plan and to implement it.

At the airport in Montgomery, commercial planes are not allowed to depart unless a flight plan has first been established. The pilot has to sit down and indicate what time the plane will leave, the route the plane will take, the altitude at which the plane will fly, the estimated time of arrival, and many other details. If planes were allowed to take off without a flight plan, and simply to fly with no destination in mind, this would have the net effect of a lot of planes in the sky going nowhere.

As obvious as this illustration is, many churches are going nowhere because they have no plan. Many congregations simply flounder like a piece of paper in a parking lot on a windy day; they just go in whatever direction the wind might be blowing. These kinds of congregations never get anywhere and run the risk of winding up in a trash bin, because they have not carried out God's purpose and plan for their existence.

If we fail to plan, we plan to fail! The church is the most important

1

institution in today's world. The church is involved in the most important journey in today's world. It is essential for the church to reach the destination God intends. For that to happen, prayerful planning is essential. And the place to begin is with the selection of your planning group.

Selection of the Planning Group

The selection of your "Joel" Committee is an extremely important process. This group will be called upon to offer many plans and visions for ministry. Some of its suggestions will be in response to potentially controversial decisions that must be reached by the Administrative Board and membership of the congregation. At Frazer, with all of our history of moving, our Joel Committee has helped us through some extremely controversial issues in a way that God has used to advance the cause of Christ.

The effectiveness of your Joel Committee will depend upon the integrity of the committee members and the leadership they display in the life of the congregation. The Joel Committee will always report in the accountability structure to the Council on Ministries and the Administrative Board. For this reason, it is essential to include the leadership from these groups. The Joel Committee is not some ad hoc group operating outside the structure of the church, but is representative of the leadership of the congregation and will report as a good steward with accountability.

At the same time, the Joel Committee represents the membership of the congregation as a whole. For this reason, at Frazer, about one-half of the members of the Joel Committee are selected because of the office they occupy in the church. This always includes the chairperson of the Administrative Board, the lay leader, the chairperson of the Finance Committee, and the chairpersons of the work areas on Education and Evangelism. The remainder of the Committee, then, is composed of members who serve in other leadership positions, and representatives from each age grouping so that all age groups are represented.

In addition, in order to make your Joel Committee as representative as possible, it is a good idea to select members who have a range of experience. Select a few people who have some expertise to offer the planning process, such as a person in real estate, or a person who has the responsibility for planning in industry as part of his or her regular vocation. Select some people simply because you perceive that they have the capacity to see the "big picture." Always select a person who has joined the congregation recently. A new member has a different perception than someone who has been a member for years. It can also be helpful to include a person who is currently visiting, but hasn't joined the congregation yet. A visitor can offer a fresh new perspective.

In all, if the members of your congregation have faith in the integrity of the leadership of your Joel Committee, they will be much more willing to accept the challenge of dreams and visions that emerge from the Committee.

Ownership of the Plan

One of the great assets of this model is that a plan is developed by lay people rather than by the pastor. Congregations that do not have some kind of planning process usually have only a pastor's plan to follow—a plan that belongs to the pastor, resides in the pastor's mind, comes when the pastor comes, and leaves when the pastor leaves. Very seldom does the plan get from the pastor's mind to the people's hands and hearts. The people certainly do not have ownership of the plan, because they had no part in designing it.

Think for a moment about what happens to lay people when the plan for their congregation moves with the pastor. A new pastor moves in, and all of a sudden a new plan is being projected. It must be awfully confusing for lay people to experience a pastoral change when there is no plan that the congregation has formulated for ministry. Every pastor seems to bring a new plan and a new set of ideas, and that can be confusing.

For this reason, the model being proposed here is an especially effective way of dealing with problems of pastoral change in an itinerant system such as that of The United Methodist Church. When the pastor moves, the plan stays, because it was developed by lay people through the Joel Committee. The pastor's role is to help implement the plan.

Of course, this whole concept underscores a strong trust relationship on the part of clergy and laity. How can the church expect to be a strong force in society, unless clergy and laity sense their mutual responsibilities in trusting each other and working closely together? I think we clergy must reevaluate the limitations we have put on the abilities and trust level of lay people. Laity have such a big vision of what God wants to do through the church and are eager to help design a plan to see God accomplish it through their congregation.

At the same time, the role of the clergy in collaboration with the Joel Committee is very important. At Frazer, as senior pastor, I have had the responsibility of recommending names for selection to the Joel Committee. This is recognized as part of my leadership responsibility. Notice, I did not say that I simply choose the members of the Committee. Rather, I submit names to the Administrative Board for their approval and election.

In addition, part of my role as pastor is to inspire and hold accountable. I always contact each member approved for selection to the Committee and stress to him/her the importance of the planning process and of each person's participation in it. I express my expectation that all members of the Committee will be present at each meeting. What we cover in each session builds upon what was covered in the previous sessions. I suggest that a person not agree to serve unless that person can attend each session. I have discovered that lay people will change their business or personal schedules to be present for the Joel Committee meetings. Lay people respond to the level of expectation that is presented to them!

Further, I always list the number of times the committee will meet—usually four to six times a year. I express confidence that the committee can do its work in this time, and I have discovered that committees usually complete their work in the amount of time that is predetermined. Committees that have no set expectation for ending usually last a longer time and accomplish very little.

Following this approach, I have discovered that lay people get extremely excited about being involved in a plan into which they have given input and design. Lay people will give all the money, time, and talent necessary to carry out a plan in which they really believe. Lay people seldom will give much commitment to a plan they perceive as the pastor trying to sell them something they need to be doing. Lay people are interested and committed if they sense that they have a part in creating the plan.

Lay people get excited about seeing God's will done through the life of the local congregation. They begin to catch a vision of what God wants to do through the local congregation and see the tremendous part they are playing in helping carry out God's will.

Ownership of the plan is a great motivation for ministry. If people have designed a ministry, they are eager to communicate that plan to the rest of the congregation. The best interpreters of the plan become the people who participated in designing it.

Scope of Planning

The Joel Committee is a short-term committee—more like a task force. The Committee is asked to serve effectively for a specific period of time and to make its report. Then it is dissolved. I personally feel that this is realistic if the individual members of the Committee do their homework and plan to complete their work at a given time.

Notice, the concrete goal of the Joel Committee is the presentation of its report to the Administrative Board of the congregation and to the Council on Ministries. The Council and the Board are then asked to review and approve the plan. Once the report is adopted, it is then published in the worship bulletin so that every member of the congregation is informed of the long-range plan.

Notice too that this process does not simply assume passage by the Council and the Board. Theoretically it is possible for the report to be rejected. But this again is where the selection of your Joel Committee plays such a vital role. The selection of Joel Committee members and the leadership and integrity they have in the congregation will largely determine the response of the accountability groups for adopting the proposals. If the Administrative Board and the congregation have faith in the Joel Committee, they will approach the report from the perspective of trust and faith. Each time a congregation adopts the proposals of the Joel Committee, and the plan is carried out, it gives greater credibility and trust to the next Joel Committee. Almost all of the Joel Committee reports from Frazer Memorial have been adopted unanimously by the Administrative Board. This is due more to the people serving on the Committee than to the proposals presented.

The basic format of presenting the report at Frazer is always the same (see the report form on page 6, and the examples of actual reports in the Appendix, pages 109-114). We always begin with the names of the members of the Joel Committee making the report. This is important. In keeping with all that we have said on this subject above, most people want to know who is involved in making proposals before they even consider the proposals themselves.

JOEL COMMITTEE REPORT
Date

Committee Members

_____   _____   _____   _____
_____   _____   _____   _____
_____   _____   _____   _____

etc.

Statistical Data

Year	Sunday School Attendance	Worship Attendance
1988	_____	_____
1989	_____	_____
1990	_____	_____
1991	_____	_____
1992	_____	_____
1993	_____	_____
1994	_____	_____
1995	_____	_____
1996	_____	_____
1997	_____	_____

Facilities
1. Recommendation based on statistics and interpretation of statistics.
2. Recommendation . . .
3. etc.

Staff
1. Recommendation based on statistics and interpretation of statistics.
2. etc.

Ministries
1. Recommendation based on statistics and interpretation of statistics.
2. Recommendation . . .
3. Recommendation . . .
4. etc.

After the Committee members are listed, our custom at Frazer has been to move immediately to a presentation of basic statistical data. First we look at the actual figures for Sunday school and worship attendance in recent years, and then we project attendance figures on that basis into the future. Listing these projections gives people a real vision of the potential of the congregation. At the time of Frazer's first Joel Committee's report, the Committee and the Administrative Board were both amazed at the potential indicated by the statistical studies. The report helped to expand the vision of everyone, and opened up possibilities for growth that we would never have imagined.

In the report for 1980, for example (see Appendix, page 111), we registered a growth trend in Sunday school that had reached 800. From there, we projected a figure of 950 in 1981 and 1,100 in 1982. The figures for your congregation would naturally have to be adjusted to reflect your own trends. If recent trends have been down, you may have to generate new ministry before your report can become a positive projection. But it is amazing how the planning process itself, grounded in prayer, can move you toward more positive results.

Notice, at Frazer, we always deal more with *attendance* at Sunday school and worship than with membership. The plans toward which we are aiming involve facilities, staff, and ministries. These kinds of plans relate more to numbers of people participating than to numbers on the membership roll.

Next in the report, based on statistics and projections, we move to the three major areas of the report itself. The scope of the planning process at Frazer centers on three areas: ministries, staff, facilities. We use the term *ministries* rather than *programs* because the church is not an institution running a program. Rather, it is a community of faith that is in ministry. Likewise, staff is essential to train and equip people for ministry; and facilities are essential to give staff and lay people a place to be in ministry.

Good planning looks at these three areas: ministries, staff, and facilities. Part of our responsibility is to be sure we plan for each of these areas to keep them in proportion to each other. The three must form an equilateral triangle.

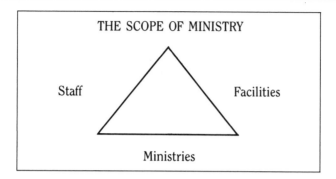

FACILITIES

Facilities and property are essential to give staff and lay people an opportunity to do ministry through the local church. Some group needs to be planning for future property and facilities. Many churches are "locked in" by property and facility limitations because of poor planning in the past. Property and facilities should not determine the scope of ministry anymore than a shoe should determine the size of the foot!

In 1980, the Joel Committee report at Frazer indicated that worship facilities should be enlarged. It also suggested that a decision should be made by the end of 1980 concerning these facilities. This put the church in a position of acting for the future rather than reacting at a time when the facilities were overcrowded. Since we were already involved in three morning worship services, the decision was made in 1980 to pursue a larger sanctuary. Architectural plans were drawn, and a new sanctuary became a reality in 1982! This was an example of the importance of planning.

One of the options for dealing with the question of additional facilities was the possibility of relocating again. These suggestions were listed in the report under "Facilities." The Joel Committee is an effective way to deal with very controversial questions. You might imagine how controversial it would be if the church had just relocated ten years earlier, and now was considering relocating again!

The credibility of the study group was so strong that the Administrative Board voted unanimously to consider the possibility of selling the current facilities and relocating. The process of planning made possible the consideration of the possibility of relocating. The major reason for remaining at the present location was the availability of additional property at the time the Joel Committee was making this report.

New recommendations were made for facilities in subsequent Joel Committee reports. In 1986, for example (see Appendix, page 113), recommendations were made to provide additional nursery space; to expand worship space in the existing building; to provide additional office space, rooms for children's ministry, and additional parking space. In the area of facilities, the needs of each congregation will naturally be different, and these needs will change and become more dynamic as years of prayerful planning build on each other.

STAFF

Staff is essential to train and equip people for ministry. The task of staff is never to do ministry, but rather to train lay people for ministry.

The recommendation concerning staff at Frazer has become a standard one. The Staff/Parish Committee is charged with the responsibility of adding a staff person as new members are received into the church. Because of the large use of part-time staff persons, the Staff/Parish Committee has the option of hiring part-time persons or a full-time staff member. The Administrative Board does not hold the Staff/Parish Committee in strict obedience to a formula based on the ratio of new members required to hire a new staff member. The Board leaves this basically up to the Staff/Parish Committee. The Board does, however, put a large sum of money into each new budget to be used for hiring additional staff persons. The figure of $50,000 is provided in next year's budget for future staff.

At Frazer, we have had a lot of discussion about how many new members will require an additional staff person. In 1980 we used the figure of 350 new members. You will notice in the report from 1986 that we had the number less defined when we said that a staff person should be hired for every 200-350 new members. The reason for this wide range is the strong commitment to utilizing part-time staff persons. Also, each part-time staff person is not expected to give the same amount of time as other part-time staff people.

One other thing we encountered as we started to grow was the need to differentiate between new members and net gain of new members. In 1980 we were not losing many new members due to their moving and transfer. By 1986 this became more critical, and is more critical today. We now use a basic rule of thumb of adding a full-time staff person or two to three part-time staff persons for every net gain of 250 members.

MINISTRIES

Facilities and staff are not an end in themselves. As we have said before, the bedrock of all planning is ministry. But it is interesting—even amazing—to observe how the plans for ministry always dovetail with the plans for facilities and staff.

This is a good place to re-emphasize the difference between ministry and program. Programs can easily become "busy work." Programs have a tendency to become self-serving and create a need to perpetuate themselves. On the other hand, ministry is serving. The model is servanthood—people finding life as they lose their lives in service. Programs tend to become "church work." Ministries are the "work of the church." People get tired of "church work," but they never get tired of the "work of the church."

In the area of ministries, several concrete suggestions were made by the 1980 Joel Committee that became reality in ensuing years. The committee suggested the use of portable classrooms for Sunday school to help meet that facility need. Those portable classrooms became a reality in 1981 and proved to be an effective way of providing facilities for Sunday school and small group needs.

Also in 1980 the Joel Committee gave visibility to the importance of assimilating new members. This task was given to the work area on Evangelism and the work area on Stewardship, in order for specific measures to be taken to insure that we were responsible stewards in assimilating new people. One specific plan that grew out of this was to have an Administrative Board member assigned to each new family unit to serve as sponsors of that new member unit. The Administrative Board member would report back concerning the place where the new member was involved in serving and the Sunday school class in which the new member was participating.

In 1986, on the other hand, a number of new and important ministries were envisioned by the Joel Committee. The "In Christ Way" ministry is a ministry of local missions that reaches out to people in need in the community. Any person who has financial needs can submit that need to a committee of lay persons. The most legitimate needs are determined and all money that has been given to this ministry is then distributed to people in need in the community. It is based on the model of Matthew 25 when Jesus talked about people who were hungry, imprisoned, naked, lonely, and said, "Just as you did it to one of the least of these who are members of my family, you did it to me" (25:40).

The In Christ Way Ministry has continued to grow. In 1990, In Christ Way Ministry gave out over $120,000 to pay utility bills, house payments, etc. An additional 6,000 families were helped with clothing; 5,394 pounds of food were distributed; and 100 family units were given financial counseling.

Another important ministry that was suggested in 1986 was the "Debt Retirement" emphasis. The Finance Committee and Stewardship Committee worked toward a plan for Frazer to become debt-free. Beginning in 1986, the money for all building needs was given before the buildings were constructed. People were given an opportunity to pledge to an early debt retirement during the stewardship program. An additional $300,000 was paid each year on the early debt retirement. Frazer should be debt-free in the early 1990s.

These illustrations are not intended to suggest that every recommendation of every Joel Committee at Frazer has gone off without a hitch. In 1980, the Committee recommended that we find ways to increase participation at the 8:40 A.M. hour both in Sunday school and in worship. Because the congregation was basically young, we had a difficult time building a strong 8:40 worship service. Young couples with small children do not get up early on Sunday morning and bring them to Sunday school or worship.

One suggestion here was to start a fellowship breakfast to encourage families to come together, meet other families, and eat before the early morning worship service. Several people volunteered to prepare the breakfast, and this is a ministry that continues to grow. Today the Sunday morning breakfast and fellowship is an important part of the total ministry of Frazer.

As you look through the sample Joel Committee reports from Frazer (given in the Appendix), you will see many more ideas for ministry that began with this Committee and its report: a counseling center, a teacher training program, the Frazer Memorial Television Ministry. (Today this television ministry involves about eighty volunteers and presents ten hours of programming each week on five different stations, including the local ABC affiliate.) The list goes on. But what is most significant is not the specific things that Frazer has done in its ministry, but what you can do if you will use an effective planning model. All of the ministries we have named began with a Joel Committee that dreamed a dream to open new doors for ministry.

Before concluding this section, I must emphasize an additional point: *the importance of carrying out the plan.* Plans are no good unless the church carries them out. I have tried to illustrate here some of the concrete ways in which Frazer has carried out the plans that were formulated by its Joel Committee. The Joel Committee dreams dreams, then gives those dreams to the appropriate committees in the congregation to work out the details, and then the congregation experiences the joy of seeing plans become reality.

A very simple formula to follow in the church is, "Plan your work— work your plan." Working the plan is as important as planning the work!

The Saul Syndrome

Before concluding this chapter, I must also emphasize an additional principle: *the importance of indigenous planning.* This has been implied in all that we have said thus far. "Indigenous planning" simply means a plan based on and tuned to the realities (statistics, facts, and possibilities) of your area and context. Though I have included illustrations from Frazer, these are not intended to suggest that you should necessarily try to do the specific ministries that Frazer has discovered. Discover those that can thrive in your context. Moreover, though this book is published by a denominational publisher, this is not intended to imply that the denominational headquarters has a plan to fit every particular situation. You must do your own indigenous planning.

On the other hand, if you will use the model described here, something great can happen. When lay people design your plan, the plan will fit your congregation. Each congregation should prayerfully plan so that the design for ministry is custom-made for each situation.

For a congregation to fail to plan for its own ministry and simply to look at somebody else's plan that might be working in another setting would be like ordering clothes from a catalog without indicating the size. Clothes could be ordered from a catalog, but if they didn't fit, the person probably wouldn't wear them. If that person *did* wear the clothes, he or she would look rather peculiar in them. Congregations that simply order programs and plans from other people usually function ineffectively and look fairly peculiar trying to wear them. When your Joel Committee designs a plan for your congregation, the plan fits. It is indigenous. The plan fits the people for the purpose God is calling them to fulfill in that given situation.

Many congregations have what I would refer to as a "Saul Syndrome." You remember how David carried the food to his brothers as recorded in 1 Samuel 17. He saw that the lines of battle with the Philistines had come down to the fact that someone would need to fight the giant, Goliath. No one from the Israelites had volunteered to go forward, so David volunteered. His brothers really didn't want him to go, but neither were they going to volunteer, so they were content to let him go.

His older brother, Saul, came to him and, in effect, said, "Let us show you how we have always fought." Saul then took off his armor and put it on David. Since Saul was much larger than David, the armor didn't fit. David must have looked awfully peculiar and funny trying to maneuver in Saul's armor.

David wisely said that he couldn't wear Saul's armor, but reached in his pouch and took out a sling. He then began to look for some smooth stones. He wanted to utilize the kind of weapons to which he was accustomed and could use. You remember that he went out and was victorious over the giant.

I believe congregations do not need to put on other congregations' armor. Some of the most damaging words a congregation can hear are, "Let us show you how we have always done it." I believe God gives to every congregation and to every individual unique gifts and talents. God wants each congregation to discover those talents and to utilize them for work in the kingdom.

Every congregation has a sling. It is far better to use a sling than somebody else's armor. God wants us to "do our homework" in discovering our smooth stones and in using them. The stones are there, if we are willing to discover them. God never sends the church on any mission without also providing everything necessary to be faithful in that mission!

This is the function of this model—to help a local church select its sling and find its stones so it can go out and be victorious in the great calling God has given to each congregation.

CHAPTER 2
DEFINE THE PRIORITIES

The next step in developing your model for growth is to come to terms with the priorities of the church. This too is a function of your planning committee. Congregations are involved in a lot of good things, but priorities must be set. Congregations do not have the resources to spend their time, energy, or money without defining priorities.

On this point, the witness of the Joel Committees at Frazer has been clear. The first Joel Committee at Frazer spent its first session seeking to identify the number one priority of the Frazer family. A lot of good things were mentioned. After the first session, people were asked to consider prayerfully what should become the stated priority of the congregation. At the second meeting the priority for Frazer was established as that of *making disciples,* that is, *evangelism.*

Biblical Base

The Joel Committee spent a whole session defining *evangelism.* The word has a lot of negative connotations with some people and many people misunderstand it. In order to communicate our priority adequately to the congregation, we felt it essential to give a clear statement of our understanding of evangelism.

In keeping with stated norms of our United Methodist tradition, we felt that our definition of evangelism had to have a biblical base. Five basic passages of scripture were identified as central for a biblical understanding of evangelism:

- Matthew 28:18-20
- Mark 16:14-16
- Luke 24:45-48
- John 20:19-22
- Acts 1:6-8

Each of these passages in the first five books of the New Testament states the mandate to make disciples and witness.

Matt. 28:18-20: And Jesus came and said to them, "All authority in heaven and on earth has been given to me. Go therefore and make disciples of all nations, baptizing them in the name of the Father and of the Son and of the Holy Spirit, and teaching them to obey everything that I have commanded you. And remember, I am with you always, to the end of the age."

Mark 16:14-16: Later he appeared to the eleven themselves as they were sitting at the table; and he upbraided them for their lack of faith and stubbornness, because they had not believed those who saw him after he had risen. And he said to them, "Go into all the world and proclaim the good news to the whole creation. The one who believes and is baptized will be saved; but the one who does not believe will be condemned."

Luke 24:45-48: Then he opened their minds to understand the scriptures, and he said to them. "Thus it is written, that the Messiah is to suffer and to rise from the dead on the third day, and that repentance and forgiveness of sins is to be proclaimed in his name to all nations, beginning from Jerusalem. You are witnesses of these things."

John 20:19-22: When it was evening on that day, the first day of the week, and the doors of the house where the disciples had met were locked for fear of the Jews, Jesus came and stood among them and said, "Peace be with you." After he said this, he showed them his hands and his side. Then the disciples rejoiced when they saw the Lord. Jesus said to them again, "Peace be with you. As the Father has sent me, so I send you." When he had said this, he breathed on them and said to them, "Receive the Holy Spirit."

Acts 1:6-8: So when they had come together, they asked him, "Lord, is this the time when you will restore the kingdom to Israel?" He replied, "It is not for you to know the times or periods that the Father has set by his own authority. But you will receive power when the Holy Spirit has come upon you; and you will be my witnesses in Jerusalem, in all Judea and Samaria, and to the ends of the earth."

Every Member Involved

On the basis of this biblical mandate, the Joel Committee developed an understanding of evangelism that included every member of the congregation. Evangelism in this sense is not a committee in the life of the church. It is the task of the entire church. Evangelism is a banner that is spread over the entire church. Every member of the church is a witness to the good news of Jesus Christ.

At Frazer, we believe that evangelism is the starting point for all of the ministries of the church. Stewardship, education, social action— all are the products of what Jesus Christ has done in the individual lives of people. Evangelism is the priority.

This is not to minimize the importance of any other ministry; it is simply to say that all ministries grow out of one's personal relationship with Jesus Christ. Stewardship and tithing are important, but people do not tithe until first their own commitment to Christ is in order. Involvement in social ministries is crucial, but the motivation must come out of what Jesus Christ has done in our individual lives and in the life of the community of faith. Evangelism is our priority.

Evangelism is the heartbeat of a vital local church. Evangelism is a mandate given to the church by Him who called the church into being. I do not want to present a narrow view of evangelism, but rather one that is a vital force in the life of individuals and in the life of the church.

Definition of Evangelism

The Joel Committee at Frazer defined evangelism as follows:

Evangelism is the proclamation by word and deed of the saving act of God in Jesus Christ to people, with a desire that they will decide for faith and become Christian disciples through the church.

That definition took a lot of time and effort by the Joel Committee, but each word in the definition is important. Let me share the understanding of that definition.

Evangelism is "proclamation by word and deed." The word *proclamation* is used because it is consistent with the root words for evangelism. The word *proclamation* is used rather than the word *preach* because preaching in today's culture usually denotes what happens behind the pulpit. Proclamation in the New Testament was what happened in the marketplace as people shared with each other concerning the event of Jesus Christ.

Proclamation is the "good news" that God has become known to us in the form of Jesus. The nature of God has been revealed to us through the Son, Jesus. "And the Word became flesh and lived among us, and we have seen his glory, the glory as of a father's only son, full of grace and truth" (John 1:14).

Proclaiming the "good news" gives witness to the reality of God. In proclaiming the "good news" a person does not give witness to some great idea, but to an event—God's event. Proclaiming the "good news" concerning the kingdom of God does not deal with ideas about God, but with the reality of God.

Proclamation is not an ideal or a set of truths to be grasped, but the personal sharing by an individual of God's grace toward that person. The validity of the proclamation is not measured in terms of success, but rather in terms of faithfulness to the biblical mandate to "witness and make disciples."

Evangelism, therefore, is what happens when lay people share with each other in their normal social contexts. Evangelism is not having a revival once a year or having some kind of special worship service. Evangelism is what happens when lay people share with each other in their natural webs of contact.

The heart of Frazer's growth is based on lay people, not clergy. Many churches have a concept that the pastor is paid to be the evangelist. But the pastor does not have the contacts with unchurched people that laity have. Proclamation is what lay people do as they engage other lay people in natural settings. Evangelism is the opportunity given to each church member.

Our definition also places the emphasis on *word and deed*. Who a person *is* oftentimes speaks more loudly than what the person *says*. Lifestyle communicates and proclaims. Actions often speak louder than words. Our proclamation is both what we say and what we do.

This understanding of proclamation as being what lay people do in their natural webs of contact is a strong affirmation of the meaning of the Bible. The Bible is a testimony of the activity of God, not restricted to the events of the Bible, but applicable to the present as well. The Bible is not only a record of the normative acts of God, but a touch-stone to show the activity of God for the present time: "Not with our ancestors did the Lord make this covenant, but with us, who are all of us here alive today" (Deut. 5:3). The Bible actually took place in biblical days, but also takes place here!

Biblical proclamation, then, is the activity of God which is not restricted to the events of the Bible, but is applicable to the present as well. Biblical proclamation is not commitment to formulated dogma of the past, but is open to God's dealing with people today as God's Word engages a contemporary situation. Through the Bible God is speaking to us today and summoning us to play our part in the redemptive plan of God for the world. Biblical history becomes our history. The Bible is not just repeating an ancient chronical of past events, but is bearing witness to the quality of the new life in Christ that people today can experience.

The Frazer definition of evangelism also includes *good news*. A lot of evangelism we hear about today is bad news, focusing on the negative—fear and intimidation. Evangelism is good news. It is the saving act of God in Jesus Christ. God initiates love toward us in sending the Son, Jesus Christ. Evangelism is not something an individual tries to do—it is simply a response to what God has already done for us in Jesus Christ.

Evangelism is not, however, just a matter of proclaiming. According to our definition it is also a "desire that people will decide for faith and become Christian disciples." This understanding of evangelism brings the hearer to a time of decision. The definition makes clear that the proclamation of the good news of God's saving activity in Jesus Christ is made with a desire that the person will respond for faith. The person proclaiming the good news is not judged by whether or not the hearer responds favorably, but is concerned with being faithful to the proclamation. We are called to be faithful, not successful!

Evangelism confronts people with the saving activity of God in Jesus Christ. The evangelist (referring to all people who proclaim the good news) does not produce this activity, but is merely a witness to it. A question mark is placed over the past, and the possibility of a new future is offered. Proclamation produces a crisis which questions the past and forces an encounter with the Lord of the future as God breaks into the present. A person can decide for faith and become a part of the kingdom of God.

Finally, evangelism aims at the making of "disciples through the church." Evangelism does not end with an initial decision to follow Christ in faith; rather, this is where the rest of evangelism begins. The Christian life is a converting process. This is why the term *evangelism*, when rightly understood, is synonymous with "making disciples." Evangelism happens as God continues to work in the lives of disciples, reaching out through them to make new disciples, and making their own discipleship ever more full and true.

Scope of Evangelism

The kind of evangelism we are describing encompasses both proclamation and presence. It is a task that belongs to all members of a congregation wherever they are at work, worship, or leisure. Because this point is so important, I want to spend the remainder of this chapter developing it in some detail.

The Bible teaches in John 3:3 that we must be "born again." Doctors in Montgomery are not allowed to deliver babies and leave them lying on the street. They would have their licenses rejected and be prosecuted for malpractice. When a baby is born, it is placed into an intensive care unit where nurses care for it. When the baby is physically well enough, the mother carries her baby home to care for it. Someone has to feed the baby, change the baby, and care for all the baby's needs.

People who decide for faith are reborn as babies. Some evangelism efforts just end there and leave them on the street, and a "baby" has no chance to survive by itself. The task of evangelism is to help people decide for faith and be reborn, then to put them into an intensive care unit where someone is going to nurture and care for them. As with a newborn baby, the goal is that the person will grow in the Christian faith until he/she becomes mature enough to become a reproducing disciple.

In the Frazer definition of evangelism, the phrase "through the church" is essential. The most effective evangelism happens through the local church. This is a structure of accountability. The congregation is designed and gifted to assume the nurturing, discipling process. The congregation becomes accountable to God for the discipling of people. This makes church membership extremely important. This means that the church has a great responsibility for each person, and each person has an ever-increasing responsibility to become involved in the whole process of making disciples.

This concept assumes that evangelism is not completed when a person joins a congregation, but that it is a part of the process of involving that person in the life of the congregation. Assimilation, therefore, is also a part of evangelism. It becomes important for the person who has made a new commitment and joined the church to become involved in a small group and in a function of ministry.

The concept for the church is really understood at two levels—the overall community of the membership of the church, and the different subgroups or "communities" that are formed around several different dynamics. Some of these small groups are based on special interests or special talents; some are sociological groups, or economic groupings, or vocational groups. It is important to be intentional about developing these small communities. The more communities created within the church, the more opportunities a person has to become a part of one of these small groups for fellowship and service. It is essential for the new member to become involved in a small group and in a function of service.

The purpose of these small groups is to minister to the world and to the community itself. The directional force of each community is both in and out. A diagram would look like this:

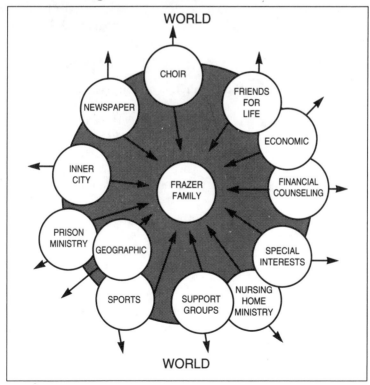

A person may be in more than one of these "communities" or small groups. Many of the communities will overlap. The important thing is for the directional interest to be both out to the world and in to the group. The purpose of the community is both for fellowship and for service.

The purpose of evangelism then is to produce disciples who by word and by deed will proclaim the good news in the day-to-day situations of life. The good news is to the whole person. This proclaiming calls and gathers people into the church. The church provides communities where the new disciple may find fellowship and service, thus authentic evangelism becomes self-propagating in the sense that proclamation produces disciples who, through the church, become proclaimers who produce disciples, and so on.

The priority is making disciples. At Frazer, we have grown to use this as a criterion for all the ministries of the church. Each ministry is evaluated yearly by the council on ministries, according to the criterion of whether or not it is making disciples. Frazer does not have the time, money, or energy to be involved in good programs that are not ministries making disciples.

*   *   *   *   *

An excellent example of this definition of evangelism in operation is seen in the lives of two people in the Frazer family. It all began when some members took very seriously the importance of carrying the good news to all people—even to those in prison. Some lay people at Frazer started a prison ministry. About eight years ago, one of the prisoners named Tommy Waites responded positively to the loving witness of the Frazer ministry. He made a commitment to Jesus Christ.

The people in the prison ministry kept going back to him and helped disciple him in the Christian faith. They knew that evangelism was not just making a decision, but helping nurture the person and giving that person an opportunity for growth. Those people cared for Tommy Waites.

Tommy was serving a life sentence. About six years later, he was up for parole. Two of the requirements for parole were to have a place to live and a place to work. The people in the prison ministry told Tommy they would help him.

After several doors closed for employment, the committee suggested that the church hire Tommy on the custodial staff. Tommy loves to describe that first day he came to the church in his prison uniform, an armed guard escorting him. He sat down with the church administrator to seek employment and Frazer hired him for the custodial staff. Tommy has no formal education, but he is a diligent student of the Bible and an excellent communicator. He loves to talk to people while he does his custodial services. Some of the Sunday school teachers asked him to come teach their classes. He became extremely popular as a Sunday school teacher. But the story doesn't end there.

About five years ago a man in Montgomery was invited to come to Frazer. He had not been to church in years. He decided to play it safe by coming on a Sunday night. We close the Sunday night worship service with an altar prayer time. Wes Strane really did not like being at church and was quite resistant. During the altar prayer time he saw an extremely handicapped young man trying to make his way down to the altar. He was holding on to each pew as he came forward. God used the scene of that young man to touch the heart of Wes Strane. He thought to himself, "That boy is crippled in body, but I am crippled in my mind."

Wes got up from his pew and helped the boy down to the altar and knelt beside him. It was there that he confronted the reality of a God who really cared for him and was calling him to be a disciple. Wes Strane made that commitment. He is an example of what can happen when people invite people to church! Wes joined a Sunday school class and became interested in the prison ministry.

One Sunday morning Tommy Waites was invited to teach a large adult Sunday school class. Wes Strane was sitting with his wife on the front row. Tommy was thanking the church for reaching out to him in prison and was describing what God had done in his life. He then said there was one particular part of his life with which God had had the most difficulty. Tommy Waites said, "One place God had a hard time changing me was in my attitude toward white policemen. I hated white policemen. But when God changed my life, he changed my attitude toward white policemen, and today I have learned to love everybody—even white policemen!"

About that time Wes Strane stood up. He asked if he might say something. He said, "I am an ex-white policeman. I didn't go to church for years until I was invited to come to Frazer. God has changed my life. The one area where God has had the most difficulty with me is in my attitude toward black prisoners. But I am here today to witness to the fact that God has changed my hatred of black prisoners into a genuine love for black prisoners."

At that point, these two guys walked toward each other and embraced in front of the class. It was the most moving lesson that had ever been taught in that room! It was an example of the results of evangelism! You cannot legislate human relationships and race relations. The answer to the prison problems lies in the kind of prison ministry that changes the hearts and attitudes of people. The answer to changing racial prejudice is in the task of evangelism, of making disciples.

Shortly after this, some lay people suggested that Tommy Waites did not need to be on the custodial staff, but should be involved in a large housing project where we wanted to start a ministry. It is the worst area of Montgomery in terms of drug use. Several different churches and organizations had tried to start ministries there, but were ineffective.

We talked with Tommy about starting a ministry there. The first person to volunteer to help Tommy in that ministry was Wes Strane! Today those two have an effective ministry in the Riverside Heights Housing Project. They utilize an abandoned church building. On Sunday mornings they have about seventy-five adults in worship and oftentimes on Sunday afternoons have over 100 boys and girls in Sunday school. They are disciples making disciples in an important ministry in that section of town.

This is why evangelism is a priority. Social concerns, stewardship, education—all grow out of the results of evangelism.

Evangelism is the heart of the church. It is the priority for the church. Every member of the church is a part of the evangelistic task of the church. Evangelism is a good word because it means "proclaiming the good news."

CHAPTER 3
DECIDE TO GROW

The third step in developing a model for growth is that a local church has to decide whether or not it *wants* to grow. This might at first glance seem like a rather simple question. I think it is the most difficult question a church has to face. It is not an easy one and it is not a question that is answered once and for all—the congregation has to answer this question every week.

Frazer has made the initial decision to grow, and we have to keep making the smaller decisions if we want to continue to grow. Even after acknowledging evangelism as priority one, a congregation must still decide to grow. Many congregations do not want to make this decision. Many congregations want to grow as long as it doesn't require any change. But there can be no growth without change. Change and the willingness to change are a part of the decision to grow.

I was recently meeting with people from a congregation who asked me to talk with them about church growth. The first question I asked was, "Do you want to grow?" The people immediately responded, "Yes." Then they started talking about the uniqueness of their church and how nearly everyone in the church was kin to someone else. All of a sudden one of them said, "We really want to grow, as long as we don't have to take in any people who are not kin to some of us." The person didn't really mean to say what he said, but he actually put his finger on the reason the church had not grown in the past and will not grow in the future.

Not a One-Time Decision

A decision to grow is not a one-time decision. Frazer made a definite decision to grow. But, we have to reaffirm that decision almost every week. Just recently the Joel Committee completed its meetings and we were looking at the need for additional property ten years from now. A church of another denomination, next door, was willing to sell us its building and property. We had already established a plan for our financial resources for the next couple of years and felt good about the plan. All of a sudden there was a possibility of needing an additional $2 million. Some of us initially were more interested in carrying out the plan we had started than making a $2 million commitment for an opportunity that God seemed to open before us. We prayed about it and decided we needed to purchase the property in order to grow in the future. We made the decision again for growth.

As we have said before, the model we are describing allows for a church to deal with some very difficult situations in a creative manner. As our first Joel Committee started to look at some projections of attendance at Sunday school and worship, we began to see that we would soon have more people attending than we had available space. This was an encouraging situation, except that we had to face the difficulties of dealing with growth. Some people looking at our situation might take the attitude that we should have kept things as they had always been instead of spending more money and building more buildings or doing things in a different manner. It became obvious to our Joel Committee, however, that we would either have to build more facilities or better utilize our space with multiple worship services.

Multiple Worship Services

At the time I am describing, Frazer had both an 8:30 A.M. and an 11:00 A.M. worship service. In view of our rising attendance, someone suggested another worship service. I thought this was good, except that I did not see a time when we could meet. Someone in the Joel Committee suggested meeting at 9:45. Someone quickly explained that we already had Sunday school at that hour and thought that would end the discussion.

The first person then suggested that we really needed more Sunday school space, so perhaps we should have multiple Sunday school sessions and move Sunday school from 9:45 to 8:30 and 11:00 and save the 9:45 hour for a worship service. That seemed logical, except that we had never done that before. Someone has well said that the seven last words of the church are, "We never did it that way before." Some of our people had never attended a worship service before attending Sunday school. A lot of us were really worried as to whether or not God could adjust to being worshiped at 9:45 and then involved in teaching at 11:00! We had never done it that way before. The church had a decision to make. Were we willing to do something different?

This also involved some Sunday school classes. People who have always come to Sunday school at 9:45 did not want to change to 8:30 or 11:00. Some of the older people had never gone to Sunday school except at 9:45. The church had a major decision. Were we willing to make some changes in order to accommodate more people and grow, or would we decide to continue with business as usual?

If this had been my idea to create all this change, rather than the plan of the Joel Committee, I probably would not have been pastor of the church long after that. I am sure they would have suggested some other place for the Bishop to send me to serve! But this was a suggestion of the Joel Committee. This was the people's plan. They had ownership of it, and they were willing to see that it would work.

It was not the pastor who went to the Sunday school classes and told them they were going to change times—it was members of the Joel Committee. Almost every Sunday school class had some member on the Joel Committee, so they went back to their own classes to tell them what we were doing. It also made great sense because everyone had been attending Sunday school at 9:45 and was already available for that additional worship service.

One key thing to remember is that when you start a new worship service, be sure you have a built-in group to make it successful. If you ever start a worship service with the hopes that some people will be there and not many are there, then the new worship service will fail. It will also be extremely difficult to try in the future to start an additional worship service. Always build in a group of people who are committed to starting a new worship service and to insuring its success. It then has a good chance to be successful and grow.

This same principle is also true for starting a new Sunday school class. Always have a group of people committed to being present the first time the new class meets. This will insure its initial success and posture it for growth and vitality. People also like to be part of something new. The result has been that our 9:45 worship service has continued to grow.

Rather than building a larger facility immediately, we went to three morning worship services. We eventually went to three Sunday school sessions. This was the best utilization of the church facilities, because every room in the church is used by three different groups on Sunday morning.

The biggest difficulty was that everybody had to change, and change is not always easy. But the more important question was deciding whether or not we wanted to grow. As long as the church can continue to answer positively the question about growth, God will always provide a way to meet every situation!

Changing Role of Pastor

I must also confess that the changing role of the pastor is an important part of the decision to grow. I have been one of the factors that has hindered growth at Frazer, because I have oftentimes not been willing to change my role.

My basic love is that of being a pastor. I love relationships with lay persons. I want to be present when people are in the hospital, or young people are being honored at school, or at the special moments in the lives of families.

As the congregation grows, a pastor cannot be every place with every person. One of my favorite worship services has been the Christmas Eve Communion service. The first few years I was at Frazer, I was able to kneel and pray with families and call the name of the mother, the father, and each child, and pray for them individually. At the last Christmas Eve service I served communion to a lot of families whose names I did not even know. My role as pastor today is entirely different from what it was ten years ago. I have to ask myself constantly whether or not I really desire growth.

Open Doors for Leadership

Another area in which the church has to decide whether or not it wants to grow is in the area of leadership. The first Joel Committee suggested that an open door for leadership was essential for growth. This meant that people would not have to be part of the church for a long time before they could be considered for leadership.

Many of the people on that first Joel Committee occupied more than one place of leadership. Some of the people had been in their places of leadership for years. One essential component in attracting new people to a church is making sure that the doors of leadership are open. Some

congregations say to people that they can join and have menial responsibilities for several years; then if they prove themselves worthy, they
can some day become a leader in the congregation. This is really
saying to people, "We don't want you to participate fully in our
congregation."

The first Joel Committee called for a policy to be established that no
person would serve in more than one place of leadership at a time, and
no person would serve as a leader for more than two consecutive years.
This created opportunities to discover and develop more leaders.

I know some churches where a person occupies the same place of
leadership for years. There are probably other people who could serve
much more effectively, and new and fresh ideas would be welcomed.
Usually the person who has been a leader in a particular area can be a
tremendous asset to another person who becomes a leader.

I believe that the policy of open doors for leadership makes better
leaders out of everyone. If a person has been chairperson of the work
area on evangelism for two years, that person then rotates out of
leadership and a new person becomes chairperson of the work area on
evangelism. The person who was the leader then serves on the committee and should be one of the best members of that committee. This
helps train new leaders and gives old leaders a place where they can
serve effectively. Leaders in the church should be servants, and the
more of the servant attitude a person has, the better leader that person
becomes.

In all of this, the fundamental question for your congregation is:
"Do we want to grow?" I have not even mentioned some other difficult
areas (for example, finances) that will have to be considered should you
decide for growth. In a way, the details don't matter. You can be assured
that growth will be difficult, irrespective of the details. In any event,
your Joel Committee must find a way to face this issue, and to trust
God for the outcome: Your church can grow, if you want it to.

CHAPTER 4
DIAGNOSE HEALTH

Importance of Diagnosis

Diagnosis of the congregation's health is essential before any suggestion for prescription can be given. Prescriptions should never be offered without doing the hard work of diagnosing need. Easy prescriptions, like advice, are usually worth what they cost. Prescription without diagnosis produces malpractice! Congregations should not engage in it anymore than doctors are allowed to prescribe without first diagnosing the problem.

When we go to a doctor for a checkup, the doctor uses various instruments to measure our heart rate, blood pressure, cholesterol count, etc. These instruments give the doctor a picture of our health. Sometimes these instruments indicate that further testing needs to be done. Where these instruments point to deficiencies or raise red flags, additional tests are pursued so that medication can be prescribed. The tests point out weaknesses in our health that can be corrected by medication or surgery.

Preliminary tests sometimes show problems that, if dealt with soon, will not develop into more serious problems in the future. Oftentimes cancer, if detected early, can be dealt with effectively. If cancer goes undetected and spreads, it can be fatal. The same is true in the life of the church. Many of our problems, if detected early, can be dealt with in a creative way. If no one is monitoring the health of the church however, things can become detrimental before they are ever confronted.

Diagnostic Instruments

One of the most helpful instruments for diagnosing the health of a congregation is a graph, an instrument that depicts trends in a local church—both healthy and unhealthy.

A graph, being visual, appeals to the modern eye. It can be quickly

31

read and analyzed. Columns of numbers are hard to deal with, but those same columns of numbers can be placed on a line graph or a bar graph and they will communicate to lay people. Graphs have a tremendous impact in our world today. Newspapers use graphs to communicate trends and newsworthy items rather than citing a series of figures. Weather and news reports on television make extensive use of graphs. Lay people today are accustomed to reading and understanding graphs, but many people do not know how to set them up. I have designed the following worksheet for use in setting up a number of graphs that can help you diagnose your congregation's health. First, fill in the information on the worksheet. This can be secured from church records. Next, plot the information on a sheet of graph paper (available wherever office and school supplies are sold).

Analysis of Graphs

The graphs I use in this book are the same graphs that were used by the first Joel Committee. I present them here because they represent the stage of diagnosis at Frazer when it was a medium-size church. As a larger congregation now, though the numbers have changed, we continue to use these kinds of graphs. I would encourage every congregation, large or small, to utilize each of the seven graphs suggested here. There are also others that a local church might devise which would help it to diagnose its health more accurately.

Place each of these graphs on a transparency for use with an overhead projector. This will allow the whole committee to view the graphs together and to analyze them. The Joel Committee will begin to see things in these graphs that one individual looking at them would possibly miss. Diagnosing the health is a team effort.

Graph 1 (p. 34) is a linear growth graph of membership for the past ten years. To properly diagnose your health today, you have to look at where you are in comparison to where you have been in recent years. Frazer Memorial had 426 members at the end of 1966, and this number had increased to 1228 by the end of 1976.

This first graph also indicates the growth pattern for Frazier had it decided not to relocate. There is actually a decrease in membership in 1967, but then a slight increase through 1970. The growth of Frazer really began in 1970, which marked the point of relocation.

WORKSHEET FOR GRAPHS

FILL IN DATES FOR PAST ELEVEN YEARS												
19	19	19	19	19	19	19	19	19	19	19	19	19

(A)

CHURCH MEMBERSHIP AS OF THE THE END OF EACH YEAR ABOVE												

(B)

SUNDAY MORNING WORSHIP ATTENDANCE AVERAGE—AT END OF EACH YEAR ABOVE												

(C)

SUNDAY SCHOOL AVERAGE ATTENDANCE AT END OF EACH YEAR ABOVE												

(D)

WAYS PEOPLE JOIN THE CHURCH LIST FIGURES OF EACH CATEGORY AT END OF EACH YEAR ABOVE												
Transfer from U. M. church												
Transfer from other denomination												
Profession of faith												

(E)

WAYS PEOPLE LEAVE THE CHURCH LIST FIGURES FOR EACH CATEGORY AT END OF EACH YEAR ABOVE												
Transfer to U.M.C												
Transfer to another denomination												
Death or Remove from roll												

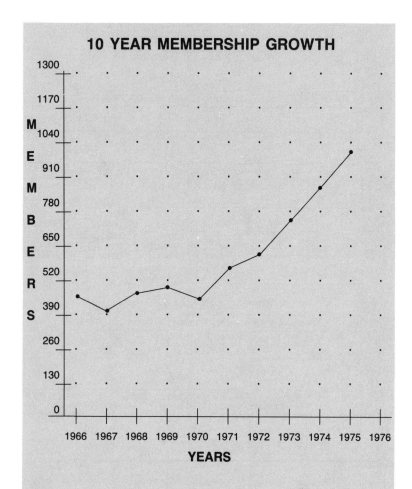

10 YEAR MEMBERSHIP GROWTH

M E M B E R S

YEARS

•MEMBERS

Graph 1

An important term and figure for discussion in diagnosing the health of the congregation is its "decadel growth rate." The decadel growth rate is the rate the church grew or declined over the past ten years. To determine the decadel growth rate, list the current membership, and then the membership ten years ago. Next, determine the amount of gain or loss, and then place the gain or loss over the membership figure for ten years ago and calculate the percentage or decadel growth rate. Below are examples of determining decadel growth rates for a growing church and a declining church:

EXAMPLE OF DECADEL GROWTH RATE

Current membership	1,000
− 10 years ago	800
10 year increase	200

From 800, the church grew by 200 members

$$\frac{200}{800} \quad = \quad 25\% \text{ gain per decade}$$

EXAMPLE OF DECADEL DECLINE RATE

Current membership	200
− 10 years ago	300
10 year loss	−100

$$\frac{100}{300} \quad = \quad 33\% \text{ loss per decade}$$

The decadel growth rate for Frazer from 1966 to 1976 was 188 percent. If you take the growth rate for the years 1971-1976, you see a decadel growth rate of 397 percent.

A linear graph will diagnose the health in a different way from a bar graph. Graph 2 (p. 36) indicates the growth of the congregation each year as compared to the previous year. This can give a different picture.

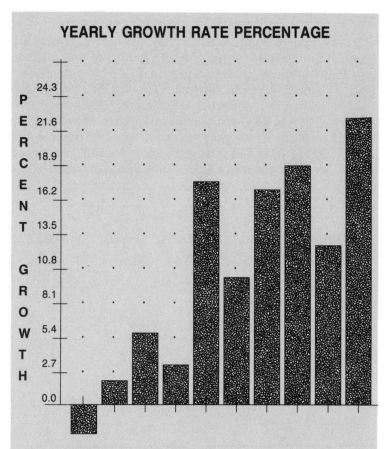

YEARLY GROWTH RATE PERCENTAGE

PERCENT GROWTH

24.3	
21.6	
18.9	
16.2	
13.5	
10.8	
8.1	
5.4	
2.7	
0.0	

1967 1968 1969 1970 1971 1972 1973 1974 1975 1976

YEARS

Graph 2

This graph illustrates that Frazer had, in most years, exceeded the growth of previous years.

The Joel Committee noted that the growth in 1969 was probably due to the completion of the building at the new site. That immediately attracted some people. The negative and minimal growth of the two previous years again point to the future of Frazer had it not relocated. The drop in the growth rate percentage for 1970 was due to the fact that the àrea to which Frazer relocated had not developed. The congregation was also in a state of readjusting to its location and had not developed any intentional, systematic plan for growth.

The bar graph indicates that the pattern was not always steady between 1970 and 1976, but there was growth taking place. One member of the Joel Committee pointed out that it is healthy to notice that a large percentage of yearly growth rate occurred within the last year plotted on the graph.

Graph 3 is a linear graph of the membership growth as compared to a projected biological growth in a decade. Biological growth is computed at 25 percent per decade and simply indicates the children who are brought up in Christian homes and usually join the church. The point of the use of a biological growth graph is that a congregation should grow at least 25 percent in a decade without any strategy for outreach. This is based on the simple fact that people have children. Oftentimes a congregation will appear to be growing, and then discover that it is only keeping up with the biological growth rate. This graph indicates that Frazer was far exceeding the normal biological growth.

Graph 3 (p. 38) is essential for congregations because it diagnoses the health based on biological growth expectations. If a congregation's membership is less than the biological growth rate, that congregation will have to take a serious look at its future and try to do further testing to see what can be done about this trend.

It is interesting to note that in 1970 the biological growth line and membership line almost intersect. Again, this indicates the pattern of Frazer had it not decided to relocate. (The slight growth from 1967 to 1970 is not authentic growth since the biological growth rate would have accounted for that much growth.)

The next two graphs indicate the means by which people are placed on a church roll, and the means by which people are taken off the church roll. The analysis of Graph 4 (p. 40) indicated a real turning

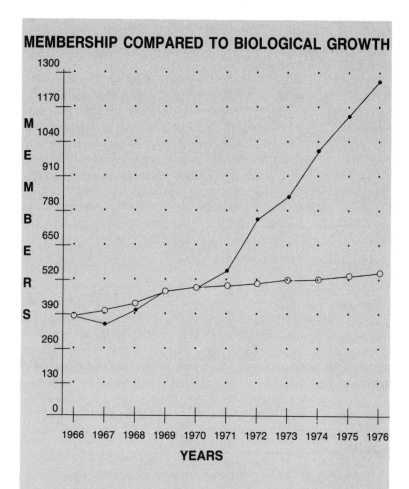

MEMBERSHIP COMPARED TO BIOLOGICAL GROWTH

• MEMBERS
○ BIO. GROWTH

Graph 3

point in the life of Frazer. I don't know of any single event that contributed more to the growth of Frazer than the study of this graph and what it communicated to the Joel Committee—and, consequently, what the Joel Committee communicated to the entire Frazer family! The analysis of this single graph, in my opinion, was more important than fifty sermons on outreach and evangelism!

In United Methodist terminology, *conversion growth* is growth whereby people join the church on confession of faith. *Reversion* indicates the number of people who withdraw their membership from the church or whose names are taken off by Charge Conference action. *Transfer in* or *out* refers to people who transfer their membership from other United Methodist congregations or other denominations. Biological *growth* and *death* are self-explanatory.

The categories of this graph apply to all denominations. However, in The United Methodist Church we consider any person a transfer who has had membership in another congregation. It might be that the person has not attended that congregation in fifteen or more years. Perhaps recently he/she had genuinely responded to God's saving activity in Jesus Christ. For the first time this person is discovering the new existence of faith. Technically, this person should come under the category of conversion growth, but in The United Methodist Church he or she will be considered transfer growth, since there was a membership in a previous congregation. Many people have experienced such a change in their lives, yet the United Methodist accounting system does not accurately account for this. Church membership and authentic faith are not always synonymous.

The other side of the coin is evident: Some young people who join through a confirmation class are considered conversion growth since they have never been a member of a congregation before. Sometimes young people are a part of a confirmation class and join just because the entire class is being received into the membership of the church. Even so, taking these kinds of ambiguities into consideration, the graphical designations for how people enter and leave the church are helpful for analysis.

The real value of these graphs became clear when the Joel Committee saw that most of our growth was coming by transfer growth. Everyone was talking about how Frazer was growing. Other people had a perception of us as a growing congregation. The "Gains by Type" graph (p. 40), however, communicated that our growth was through

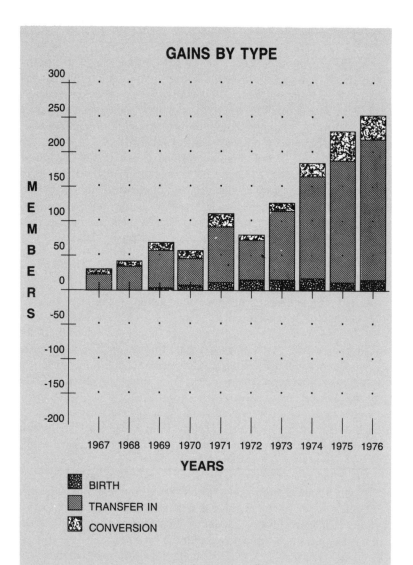

GAINS BY TYPE

BIRTH

TRANSFER IN

CONVERSION

Graph 4

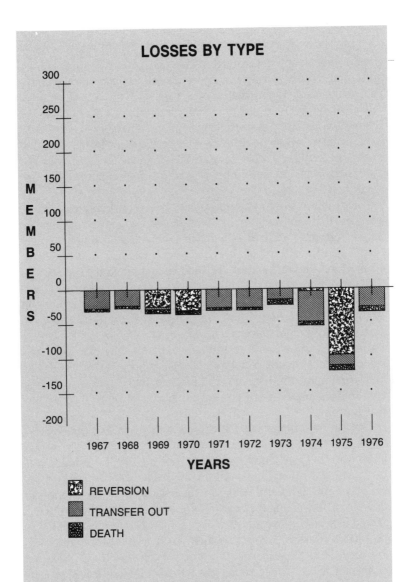

Graph 5

transfer growth and not through conversion growth. We were doing a good job of receiving people by transfer, but a very poor job at winning people who were unchurched.

The "Gains by Type" graph communicated to our people. The Joel Committee became concerned about the small number of people who were being received on conversion growth. They talked about it, prayed about it, and went back to their Sunday school classes and groups and began to make other people conscious of our call to reach unchurched people.

The diagnosis of our congregation at this point indicated a severe weakness that was caught in its infant stages. Had Frazer continued to have a perception of itself as a growing congregation simply because people were transferring in, it would never have become a strong force for reaching the unchurched. This graph communicated the point to the laity of Frazer, and they decided to do something about it. This is why, I believe, the graph was far more important than fifty sermons on evangelism would have been. *The people saw the need and were motivated to do something about it.*

All of this came home to me rather dramatically one day. I was talking with a church secretary and asked about her husband. She informed me that he worked with Purolator Courier. I wasn't familiar with that organization and asked about it. She explained the nature of that business.

That very morning I left the church building to visit the hospital. About three blocks from Frazer I stopped at a red light. Next to me was a van with the sign "Purolator Courier" on the side. I was impressed. Later, as I was proceeding down the interstate, another truck passed me and I saw printed broadly on the side of the truck, "Purolator Courier." After visiting the hospital, I stopped at a red light downtown, and all of a sudden I saw a truck pass in front of me with a sign on it, "Purolator Courier." My first reaction was that Purolator Courier had just moved to Montgomery that morning and had all these trucks out on the streets! It dawned on me that Purolator Courier had been there a long time, but I had just never "seen" the trucks. Having a person on the church staff whose husband worked with Purolator Courier helped me "see" something that had been in front of my eyes all the time!

A diagnostic tool such as a graph can help us "see" things that ought to be very obvious to us, but have not been evident to us in the past.

This graph caused lay people to "see" something that became vital to the health of the congregation.

From the analysis of the "Gains by Type" graph, Frazer began an intentional effort to reach unchurched people. Goals were set for reaching people on profession of faith. People began to pray about this, and to become conscious of the need to invite unchurched people to Frazer. The result is that Frazer quickly became one of the leading congregations in the denomination in reaching people on profession of faith.

The Southeastern Jurisdiction instituted an event to recognize the congregation that received the most people on profession of faith, and gave this congregation an award. Because Frazer won that award the first three consecutive years, it was placed in a different category in order to recognize other churches. The results of diagnosing our health in this area, and the dramatic and intentional effort to correct the symptom, are continually evident in the life of Frazer's emphasis on reaching the unchurched. In 1990, almost one-third of all the people who joined Frazer, joined on profession of faith!

Graph 6 (p. 44) breaks down the areas of how people transfer into the church. We make two distinctions—those who come from United Methodist churches and those who come from other denominations.

This graph is important because studies show that unless a congregation receives large numbers of persons from other denominations, that congregation has probably plateaued or is declining. This in no way indicates that we should proselyte from other denominations, but it does point to a modern trend—people are not denominationally oriented. They do not choose a congregation based on denomination. They pick a congregation that meets their needs. If most of the people transferring into a congregation come from that same denomination, that congregation will probably be in trouble in the future.

Our graphs have shown in recent years that more and more people are transferring from other denominations. In 1990 Frazer had a larger number of people transfer from other denominations than from other United Methodist churches!

This means of comparing how people are received by transfer pointed to a basic ingredient of the future plan for Frazer: Most of the people coming from other denominations (30 percent) were coming from one neighborhood, Arrowhead subdivision. It became evident

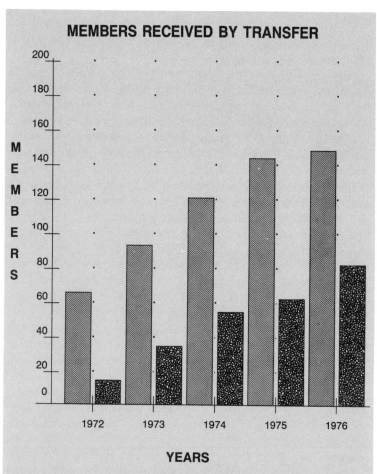

MEMBERS RECEIVED BY TRANSFER

YEARS

FROM OTHER UNITED METHODIST CHURCHES
FROM OTHER DENOMINATIONS

Graph 6

that residents of that subdivision were having more social contact with Frazer people than with people of their own denomination. As a result, they were likely to receive an invitation to attend Frazer as soon as they moved into the neighborhood. This led the Joel Committee to recognize a basic principle that has since become a byword at Frazer: *People bring people.* The congregation is growing because people are inviting people in their natural network of contacts.

This also led to a suggestion that we plot our membership on a map of Montgomery. This would help us see other patterns of growth, and it would give a good view of where our members are living. The large number of people living in Arrowhead was prominent on the map. We discovered that we had 89 families living on one street in that subdivision! We also discovered that we had 125 families in the subdivision of Arrowhead! The growth of the congregation in that area was directly due to the principle that people bring people.

The map also showed another interesting street in another neighborhood. We noticed that our congregation had six families on one short street, Edinburg Drive. The neighborhood did not have driving patterns that brought its people by Frazer, and was not a neighborhood that had a homeowners' association. It did not have any of the factors operating in it that made Frazer so appealing to the Arrowhead Community, except that the first people who moved to that street joined Frazer, and consequently began inviting other people as houses were built and people moved in. This set a trend in that neighborhood.

We also noted that there were two other United Methodist congregations near that neighborhood. Because of the location of other United Methodist congregations there, Frazer had made no intentional efforts in reaching that neighborhood. However, the principle of personal contact had a definite impact.

What happened in the Arrowhead Subdivision and on Edinburg Drive substantiates the claim that personal contact is the best means of evangelism. These points of contact within the natural web of social contacts is the best means of proclaiming the good news. The response in these neighborhoods to the witness and invitation of Frazer members is a sign of God's prevenient grace, already active in the lives of people to whom the witness was made.

People bring people—that has become the key. People are more likely to attend a church to which they are invited than simply to go to one of their own denomination. People respond much more readily to

PEOPLE BRING PEOPLE!

Last Fall I placed a chart on the front of the bulletin entitled, "Are You Inviting?" It was developed by Herb Miller of the NET RESULTS RESOURCE CENTER. It listed 9 different categories of people in the community with whom you and I cross paths. You will remember that I asked you to write in names under each of those categories, and then invite those people to attend Frazer. While I was talking about it in worship, the TV cameras presented a close shot of the chart.

A couple, Carl and Burma Rutherford, had just moved back to Montgomery after living in Florida for 32 years. They were watching the Worship Service on TV on their first Sunday back in Montgomery. When Carl saw the chart, he said to his wife. "I'll bet somebody writes our name down and invites us." His wife, Burma, laughed and replied, "Don't flatter yourself—nobody even knows we've moved back."

That very Sunday afternoon a member of Frazer knocked on their front door. He had written down their name in the category of "New people who have moved into the neighborhood." Carl answered the door. The visitor introduced himself and told him why he was there and wanted to invite them to Frazer.

I wish I could have seen Carl's face! He immediately called his wife and said, "Burma, come to the door! You won't believe what is happening. I told you so!" The Rutherfords visited Frazer the very next Sunday. They joined Frazer on February 10, 1991.

People bring people! Eighty-six percent of the people who come to Frazer, come because somebody invites them to attend. Fifty percent of the people in Montgomery are unchurched. Half of them have never received an invitation to attend a church in the Montgomery area. There are a lot of people waiting for your invitation.

Frazer has excellent visibility, accessibility, location, ministries and programs, television, radio, and a lot of other positive things to attract people—but nothing is as effective as a personal invitation. You are God's plan for His church. Each member of Frazer has an opportunity each week to bring people to Christ and to the church. People bring people!

See you at the "inviting" place Sunday!

—John Ed

(From a Frazer Memorial worship bulletin)

a personal invitation than they do to advertising, telephone campaigns, television, etc. Analyzing the "Members Received by Transfer" graph helped our committee formulate a vital part of our basic plan.

People bring people: At Frazer, we look for ways to affirm the importance of this truth. When people come forward and join the church, I ask the people who invited them to come stand with them. This affirms the lay person who invited them and communicates to the congregation that people are bringing people. This gives everybody permission to invite other people. This is also reinforced through the weekly church bulletin and other means of communication. The story on page 48 shows how this came through in one of my recent articles for the front of the church bulletin.

Graph 7 (p. 48) shows the "Average Annual Growth Rate" in the areas of membership, morning worship, Sunday school attendance, composite membership, and finances. These areas are compared for two periods: the ten-year period from 1966 to 1976, and the five-year period from 1971 to 1976. The purpose of this graph is to compare the involvement of persons with the number of those who are becoming members. A church makes no progress if people come in the front door of the church, then go right out the back. This graph is important to indicate the health of the church in the process of *assimilating* members in the discipling process.

Composite membership refers to the sum total of the church membership, the average morning worship attendance, and the average Sunday school attendance, divided by three. Since some churches have active and inactive rolls, and others keep membership figures in other ways, composite membership is the most accurate way of measuring membership.

This graph indicated that the membership and composite membership rates at Frazer were just about the same. It also pointed out a surprising problem that existed in Sunday school attendance: We were doing a poor job of involving people in Sunday school. This again led to a focused effort on starting new Sunday school classes, making Sunday school more meaningful, and inviting people within the congregation to become involved in Sunday school.

This is another illustration of how diagnosing the health of the congregation through this model can prove to be more important than preaching fifty sermons on the importance of Sunday school. Lay people diagnosed the health and decided to do something about it:

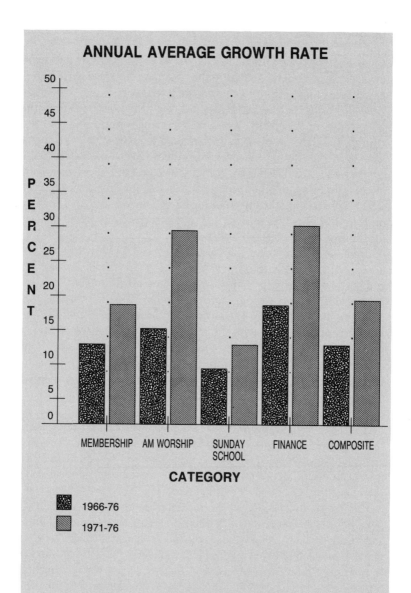

ANNUAL AVERAGE GROWTH RATE

Graph 7

Today Frazer Memorial has the largest Sunday school attendance in The United Methodist Church.

Part of the reason for the slow growth in Sunday school was the lack of facilities. This led to a plan for providing additional Sunday school space, and better utilization of the current facilities. It also led to the creative use of some portable classrooms that provided a lot of space at a relatively low financial investment. And it helped us to emphasize how important it is for persons to become part of a small group in which they can experience both fellowship and teaching.

Another interesting feature of this graph was the indication that the average growth rate of morning worship attendance at Frazer exceeded that of membership. This is dramatically illustrated in the five-year period when morning worship attendance rose at an average rate of 28.8 percent as compared to 17.4 percent in membership. Part of the reason for this growth in the morning worship attendance was that we dealt with the problem of facilities for worship before we dealt with the problem of facilities for Sunday school.

When Frazer relocated to the present site, the people made a strategic decision. While some thought we should increase Sunday school space first, a decision was finally reached to create more worship space. We noted that people usually attend worship before they attend Sunday school. In our culture people seem to want to remain anonymous at first, to "check out" a church. This can be more easily accomplished in worship than in a small Sunday school class.

Another reason for the growth of morning worship attendance was a deliberate effort to design a service of worship that was relevant to the needs of people today. A subcommittee analyzed the order of worship and the component parts of worship, and made suggestions for the elements that were most meaningful to people. Much of our previous order of worship had to be changed because it did not meet the needs of the people we were trying to reach.

The "Growth Rate" graph also allows you to diagnose the commitment level of people attending your congregation. In both the ten- and five-year periods, the increase in financial giving at Frazer exceeded all other areas of growth. A high growth rate of financial giving and attendance at morning worship services is a healthy indication of areas of commitment and involvement on the part of new people—they are not simply placing their names on the membership roll, but are becoming involved.

One of the reasons for an increase in financial giving at Frazer was the congregation's involvement in building programs. The largest increases in financial giving occurred in 1971 and 1974 when the two phases of our building program were in progress. Nevertheless, the Joel Committee felt that financial giving was more related to the commitment and involvement level of people than simply to the introduction of a new building. They also saw that the involvement of the people in the life of the congregation was directly related to their financial giving. This was an important insight and illustrated the importance of involving lay people in the total ministry of the church.

Goal Setting

Goal setting is extremely important. I would rather set a high goal and work toward it—even if I come up a little short—than to have no goal at all. At least I will have made some progress. If I have no goal, I shoot at nothing, and usually hit it!

One of the things that the Joel Committee suggested on the basis of these graphs was that Frazer set specific goals in certain areas of ministry. The work area on evangelism, for example, was asked to submit goals for new members, for persons received on profession of faith, for average worship attendance, and for average Sunday school attendance.

Some people complain that a congregation should not set goals in evangelism. I disagree. Nearly every congregation I know sets goals for the budget and for its financial responsibilities. Congregations widely publish these goals. Some congregations even display a large visual thermometer that shows the progress made toward pledging the budget. The intention is that every member of the congregation will know what the budget is, and what progress is being made toward reaching the goal of pledging the budget.

I propose that people are more important than money! We set goals for money because we think it is important. I think we should set goals for winning people to Christ and his church. Such goals need to be set by the lay people, moreover; when they have ownership of the goals, they will commit themselves to the ministries that will achieve them.

One graph that could be important in this regard shows the projected goals for congregational growth. This graph might feature the goal that is set for the year, as well as a month-by-month update of the progress toward the goal. A church could also set a ten-year goal and plot the annual progress toward reaching that goal.

Goal setting is an exercise that is understood by lay people and is an instrument for diagnosing the health of the congregation. Lay people are willing to set big goals. In fact, I have discovered recently that many of the lay people at Frazer have a far greater vision for their church than I. At its first meeting in 1990, the Administrative Board spent some time talking about the last decade of the century and where Frazer should be as a church in the year 2000. Much to my surprise, the Board suggested and voted for a goal of 20,000 members by that time! That's a huge vision—one I at first found a bit intimidating, but then I remembered something I had heard a long time ago: "It's a lot more fun trying to restrain fanatics than it is to resurrect corpses."

Another graph that we now use at Frazer, and consider to be essential, indicates the number of first-time visitors. Our overall evangelism plan is predicated on the premise that people bring people. People invite friends to worship, then the work area on evangelism follows up on those first-time visitors. Our graph will indicate whether the numbers of first-time visitors are increasing or declining. The number of people who will be joining in the months ahead is directly correlated to the number of people visiting now. It is important to be aware if your number of visitors begins to decline, so that some remedy can be found for dealing with the situation before it becomes severe.

Many other graphs can be devised to help people take a closer look at their congregation. The important thing is to diagnose problems and to do something about them early. It is also good to see the strengths of the church and to amplify these. Graphs are nothing more than a means of diagnosis. Remember, prescription before diagnosis is malpractice. Too many congregations want to prescribe without doing their homework on the diagnosis. Once the diagnosis is properly made, the prescription can move from obsolescence to real relevance.

CHAPTER 5
DOCUMENT DEMOGRAPHICS

The next step in developing your model for growth is to gather data on who the church is trying to reach. It is important to have data concerning current population and population projections for your area. Today there is more demographic data available to us than most of our congregations ever use.

Availability of Data

Where can you go to acquire demographic data? Consider a few examples from our experience at Frazer. The city of Montgomery has a Department of Planning and Development which makes projections for the future population. There is also a Central Alabama Regional Planning and Development Commission which provides various kinds of data. Some other good sources of demographic data include the Board of Realtors, the Chamber of Commerce, and the Home Builders Association. In addition, many denominations now have demographic data available by census tracts.

At Frazer, we have found that some of the most accurate information is secured from the Montgomery County Board of Education in the form of school site studies. These studies are helpful because they include both city and county, and combine these two without studying them separately. Also, they form the basis of the projections for new schools in the next few years. This allows us to see the "big picture" of population trends.

Our Joel Committee makes transparencies of the population projections and studies them. Oftentimes there is a need to break down population projections into census tracts near the church building. We generally look at both a three-mile and a five-mile radius for the census tract population projections around the church. This gives an indication of what the congregation can expect in the future.

A congregation needs to define its understanding of its own scope of ministry. Some congregations are rural; they minister in sparsely populated areas. Other congregations are downtown and require a different strategy for ministry. Some congregations minister basically in well-defined neighborhoods. Others are located near traffic arteries, have good visibility and accessibility, and serve people from larger geographic areas. A traffic impact analysis can be used to show what kind of driving distance can be expected of people who attend a specific congregation.

Implications of Data

When Frazer's first Joel Committee began studying the population projections, we discovered that Montgomery was growing at a minimal rate, and that most of this growth would occur in the section of the city where Frazer was located. We did our homework and discovered the reason for this. Montgomery is basically bordered on the north by the Alabama River, on the west by Maxwell Air Force Base, and on the south by a flood plain area; this leaves the eastern section of town the most open for future development. One study from the school board indicated that the six census tracts to which Frazer ministers could possibly increase by 40,000 people in the next fifteen years.

Naturally, the demographic data for each situation will be different. Not all congregations are located at the center of a rapidly growing area. Your congregation might even be located in an area of population decline. The point of demographic data, however, is to get in touch with the facts of each situation, whatever those facts may be.

The demographic data at Frazer proved extremely helpful to us in discovering not only how many, but who would be represented in most of this growth. I had always heard that growing churches had big youth programs. As a result I was quite frustrated that our youth program was not as large as I thought it should be. It was a source of irritation to a lot of us that we felt we were not effective in youth ministry.

As we started to gather the demographic data and to discover the breakdown of the population, we found that 66 percent of the kids in our census tract areas were in elementary school, 17 percent in junior high school, and 17 percent in senior high school. When we analyzed our Sunday school, we discovered that we were reaching a much greater percentage of the junior and senior high population than of the elementary age children. We had a much better youth ministry than we realized when we discovered who lived in our area. This also pointed to a great deficit in our ministry to children. The demographic data helped us wake up to where our greatest potential for ministry really was.

Demographic data can also indicate the family makeup of the people in the parish area. Frazer discovered that the percentage of population consisting of retired people in the Montgomery area was 16 percent. In our census tract areas, the percentage was only 6 percent. This was further indicative of the youthful age of the people in our area. It is usually younger people who move to new areas of growth and assume 30-year mortgages on their homes.

We also discovered that the percentage of people renting their homes in the Montgomery area was 40 percent. In our census tract areas the percentage of renters was only 20 percent, indicating that we were in an area where people were ready to put down "roots" even though they might be here for a short time. This also indicated a greater willingness of people to make commitments even if they are short-term, and, hopefully, a willingness of people to become involved in the life of the church, even though many of them were in the military or worked for large industries and knew they would move in the near future.

Again, the point of these examples is not simply to recall and celebrate Frazer's story, but to show the kinds of data that we found were available, and to suggest just a few of the uses to which this kind of data can be put. Get the facts on your area, and spend some significant time in your Joel Committee thinking about what this information implies for your ministry.

One surprising bit of information that came from our demographic data was the fact that Montgomery County has one of the highest median school years completed by persons twenty-five years or older of any county in Alabama. The median school years completed by people in Montgomery County is just over twelve. The median in the area Frazer serves is almost fourteen years. This means that Frazer is serving in an area that has one of the highest education levels of any area in the state of Alabama! This demographic data pointed us to the importance of a ministry designed to reach people who are well educated—persons with ties to Auburn University at Montgomery, Huntingdon College, Alabama State University, Alabama Christian

College, Troy State University of Montgomery, and Maxwell Air Force Base.

Other demographic data that we were able to acquire indicated the economic level, salary, and number of persons living in each household. All of this was important input as we started to design specific ministries.

At Frazer, this data pointed out immediately that the Joel Committee needed to look closely at the use of our facilities for the future. Along with the population projections, we began to project what we could expect in Sunday school and worship for the next ten years. It became obvious that some plans would have to be made for additional facilities.

Vision of Possibilities

One of the real assets of this exercise in diagnosing health and assessing demographic data is that it gives people a vision of the possibilities of what their congregation can be. Your Joel Committee's eyes can be opened to the immense possibilities in your area for ministry in the future. A congregation can begin to envision where it could be in the next ten and twenty years.

In a very practical way the demographic data gathered by that first Joel Committee indicated that Frazer would need more land. The church was located on five acres. During this time of study, nine acres adjacent to the church property became available. Based on the recognized and substantiated need, the church purchased the land.

In 1982 the Joel Committee was meeting and making its projections for the future and it became evident that additional property would be needed in the 1990s. The very week the Joel Committee proposed its report to the Administrative Board, a "For Sale" sign went up on ten additional acres adjacent to the church property. It looked like God's perfect timing for our planning. The church purchased those ten acres.

In 1990 the Joel Committee was again meeting and making projections for the year 2000 and beyond. God was giving a much bigger vision for growth. Again the congregation was struggling with whether or not plans should be made to relocate in the future to secure additional property because we were now surrounded by developed property. At the very time the Joel Committee was meeting, the

Landmark Church of Christ, located next door, approached the Frazer family with the possibility of buying its six acres and 26,000 ft.^{2} of building, in order that it might relocate. Frazer voted to purchase the buildings and property.

I cannot overemphasize the importance of planning. If the Joel Committee had not been meeting, in none of these cases would the congregation have ever begun to think about the importance of the future and what the needs would be. It is still amazing to all of us how God seemed to make additional property available as we began to perceive the need for it.

Act—Not React

We oftentimes use the phrase, "Act, don't react." Acting usually brings something positive. Reacting usually brings something negative. Planning allows a church to be in a posture of acting for the future. Lack of planning leaves the church in a posture of reacting. Projections for the future usually allow the church to act in a positive manner. Reaction usually causes dissension and disruption.

It is not by accident that we named the Joel Committee after the prophet Joel. Someone needs to be dreaming God's dream and seeing the vision of possibilities for God's church. But visions of possibilities need to be continually informed by facts and hard data. Documenting your demographic data will give you and your Joel Committee a solid foundation from which to dream your dreams for ministry.

CHAPTER 6
DETERMINE NEEDS

Once a congregation has decided to grow, designated its planning group, defined its priorities, diagnosed its health, and documented the demographic data, the next step in designing a model for growth is to determine the needs of the people living in the area the congregation seeks to serve. Ministries and strategies of evangelism should always be based on need. We have followed a very simple principle at Frazer—discover the need, then design a ministry to meet that need.

Ministries Based on Needs

As we saw in the last chapter, Frazer's demographic data indicated that we were surrounded by people with small children. While most of our focus had been on youth, we had greatly neglected our ministry to children and young families. The Joel Committee discovered this need, reported it to the Council on Ministries, and asked them to design such ministries. One suggestion was that we begin a children's church service, a worship service designed for the age level of children.

Children's church worship service at Frazer is quite different from the adult worship. Instead of a twenty-minute sermon, the children's church sermon usually consists of about five short sermons in the form of an object lesson, puppets, story, etc. The children's choir sings for its own worship service. The children participate in the worship service. Children's church is not an extension of a Sunday school session. It is a worship experience designed for worship at the level of each age group. It is a way for the children themselves to participate, and participation in ministry and worship is an important principle.

Offering a children's church worship service also provides an option for adults. The children's church worship services are held simultaneous with the 9:30 worship services in the sanctuary. If a family has a third grade child, that family has a choice of having the child worship with them in adult worship or allowing the child to go to a worship service for third graders. We have discovered that most children prefer the children's church worship experience.

The children's church became so popular at Frazer that we had to initiate other children's churches at the same hour. Today, during the 9:30 worship service, there are thirteen children's church worship services held simultaneously on the Frazer property! Each of them is a worship experience, yet distinctively different because of the age group to which it is ministering.

People sometimes ask where we get enough volunteers to staff these services. The fact is, since these services really meet a need of children and their parents, people look upon these times' as opportunities to serve in a creative way.

Remember now, all of this began when the good intentions of a pastor and his congregation to concentrate on youth ministry were refocused by the hard facts of demographic data. Looking closely at the data, we saw that the needs of our community pushed us to concentrate our efforts in a different direction.

Based on this same data, the Joel Committee at Frazer also determined that we needed a weekday kindergarten for four- and five-year-olds. This was pursued by our education committee, and a kindergarten was initiated.

The kindergarten has developed such a good reputation that the Montgomery community regards it as one of the finest in the city. When registration opens in February for the school enrollment for the following September, people stand in line and the kindergarten is completely filled the first morning, with a waiting list of over 100 children. Our current capacity is 350 children.

One important principle at Frazer is that any ministry should be done well or not done at all. If you are going to provide a kindergarten, provide one of the best kindergartens in town. Do your ministry with excellence.

We probably receive thirty families a year who come to the church through the kindergarten. It is unapologetically a Christian kindergarten. Christian principles are incorporated into the basic purpose of providing a learning atmosphere for children to prepare them for first grade. There is a chapel program each week for all the kindergarten children. Most of the songs they learn are Christian songs. They learn the alphabet through Bible verses that begin with the different letters of the alphabet.

Another way the Frazer family responded to the need for ministry with children was through the development of a graded children's choir program. Children love to sing, so our music department was asked to develop a program to meet this need. Today there are fourteen children's choirs that meet on Sunday evening. One or two of the choirs sing at the evening worship service each Sunday night. There are two major children's choir productions each year—one at Christmas and one in the spring. The children's choir has become a major feeder program for the youth choir and the adult choir. Here was a need, and a ministry was developed to meet it.

But the needs-based ministries at Frazer have not only been for children. The demographic data that we acquired also indicated that 51 percent of the people in the Montgomery area were single, representing the largest segment of the population. Yet Frazer had no effective ministry to singles.

Recognizing this need, a committee was formed to develop such a ministry. This group did its homework in studying how to minister to singles and initiated a singles ministry. Today there are three singles Sunday school classes that meet on Sunday morning with an average attendance of 350. Each of those classes meets for Bible study during the week and for other fellowship and outreach activities. The ministry has grown to the point that we now have a full-time singles minister, with a part-time assistant.

From the singles ministry has developed a series of needs-based support groups on Tuesday nights: support groups for people who are recently divorced, have lost a spouse to death, need financial counseling, are divorced parents with children, etc. On Tuesday nights, thirty support groups meet, with about 250 people participating. In this way, our ministry has become an outreach to singles in the city.

Likewise, if you are going to truly base your ministries upon documented needs, you will also have to take into account the fact that— over time—*needs change*. In the early studies of our demographic area we discovered there were few needs for ministry to older adults. Most of the folks moving into the new sections of the city were younger people. A recent Joel Committee has discovered, however, that in the 1990s more older adults are moving to our parish area of responsibility. This presents a tremendous opportunity for ministry, as this represents a trend in the American population: People are living longer and longer. The need to minister with older adults is becoming a priority. The Council on Ministries has been studying this need and designing ministries to meet it. We have a part-time staff person working in older adult ministry. We have started an older adult choir called "The Speeders" (over 65). Several events for older adults are planned each week. This provides opportunities to come to the church, enjoy fellowship, and focus on a Bible study together. Many of these older adults live alone and this is one of the highlights of their week.

We also discovered that one of our older adults wanted to become involved in the ministry of driving the church bus. He was a basically inactive member, but became interested in the activities for older adults. Today he has taken the church bus as his project. He drives it every Sunday morning to pick up older adults, and drives it several times during the week for special ministries. Also, he is personally responsible for the maintenance of the vehicle. The bus has become his ministry. When needs are discovered and met by a ministry, you also discover many people who have interests and talents they can contribute to that ministry.

How Ministries Develop

The concept of determining needs allows ministries to develop from the ground up rather than from the top down. Ministries that are meaningful are not ministries that staff people suggest; they are ministries that lay people identify and commit themselves to provide.

An example of this occurred four years ago when a group of people discovered that many children are born in Montgomery who are developmentally delayed or have handicapping conditions. There were few resources in the community to help the families of these children. The need was expressed to the Council on Ministries. The task of designing the ministry was then given to the Family Ministries coordinator and the Nursery Ministry.

From this need a ministry was designed which is now known as "Frazer's Friends for Life." It is basically a ministry of support to parents and children with special needs. We discovered that these parents are often afraid to leave their children in a church nursery because no one is trained to care for children with special needs. We also discovered that many of the parents are afraid to leave their child with a babysitter.

Part of the development of Friends of Life was to train babysitters who could go into the homes and care for these kids. Also, a special nursery was set up on Sunday morning for children with special needs. The need was met and the ministry started to grow. On a February Sunday morning in 1991, Friends for Life placed an insert in the worship bulletin (see page 66). This insert shows how the ministry was conceived by lay people, created and implemented by lay people, and how it is touching the lives of hundreds of people throughout the Montgomery area. Friends for Life is another example of how ministries are designed to meet needs.

Needs will always surface if the church is listening. As Frazer became involved in a strong singles ministry and in a ministry to children of divorced parents, a mother one day presented a perceptive need. She felt she was fairly effective as a mother, but in her single-parent household, her children had no firm concept of the role of a husband and father in the home. She felt strongly that an important element was missing in the life of her children.

She expressed this concern to some lay people, and they brought the issue to the Council on Ministries. The idea was given to Family Ministries and Singles Ministries, who were asked to investigate this need and see if a ministry could be designed to meet it. It was decided that an announcement should be placed in the worship bulletin stating the need and making available the opportunity for couples to "adopt" a child of a single parent in order to spend more time with that child each month, invite the child for a meal in their home, and sit with the child and the single parent at the Wednesday night dinner (see announcement, page 67).

The basic posture of Frazer is to present the need and see if people volunteer for the ministry to meet that need. In addition to the announcement, we asked one of our single parents to give a brief witness at the worship service stating the need and explaining the possibilities for ministry to this need. That Sunday forty-seven families volunteered for the ministry!

A very touching thing was waiting for me on my desk when I arrived at church on Sunday morning. A copy of the worship bulletin making the announcement of the need was lying on my desk. The part of the

FRAZER'S FRIENDS FOR LIFE

Behold, how good and how pleasant it is for people to dwell together in unity. —Psalm 133:1

Established in 1987 with eight members, Friends for Life is a ministry which has grown to more than 350 members. We offer love, support and information to families of children with special needs. Meetings are the third Tuesday of each month at 7 p.m. in the Narthex.

Friends for Life offers hope to parents of special needs children by providing meals, visitations and continued contact with that family. For more information please call 272-8622 or 277-2285.

The community of God extends beyond the doors of churches. It encompasses your homes and communities, and all the people who live there.

As members of God's Community, we become his instruments—visible proof of His love and compassion.

Like anyone else, people with special needs need love and compassion. In Alabama there are 115,000 handicapped children receiving services and this number is rising. One in every 14 children born in the U.S. has a birth defect.

There are many things we do here at Frazer that include our people with special needs in our daily lives.

—FFL offers love to families by visitation, meals, information packets to NICU patients and staff.

—We offer respite care for families through Parents Night Out once a month for 25-30 children.

—There are over 150 books in our "resource library".

—Our Equipment Loan Bank houses over 50 pieces of adaptive equipment that can be checked out to help meet the needs of special children during various stages of development.

—Our special children are mainstreamed with other children in Sunday School, Vacation Bible School and choir.

—Many members represent Friends for Life by serving on local and state councils relating to handicapped children.

—We've joined with Montgomery Junior League to present "Kids On The Block" puppets program to educate area 3rd graders about disabilities fostering an atmosphere of understanding and acceptance for disabled persons.

—We want to be the instrument of God's love and make a positive difference in the lives of others.

—Please pray for us throughout the year. With your prayers, OUR GOALS ARE LIMITLESS.

FAMILIES CARING TO SHARE

One of the joys of Frazer is how individuals volunteer to do ministry. This is the avenue through which all new ministries develop. Recently a new member indicated that she felt God was calling her to help bring together children of single parent families with married couples. She shared that as a single parent her children see what a father looks like and what a mother looks like but never what a husband and wife look like. The purpose of the new ministry would be to have children of single parent families see a role model for positive husband-wife relationships. Who should be involved as couples: Young couples without children, young couples with children, not-so-young couples with children, and not-so-young couples without children! In other words, this is for married couples who would desire to have their marriage be a ministry. Of course we want single parents who have a desire for their children to see positive husband-wife relationships. You may be interested but not sure. Let us have your name and we will invite you to an informative meeting regarding this ministry. At that time you can decide if this ministry is for you.

Name _____ Phone _____

Address _____

_____

SINGLE PARENT FAMILY   MARRIED COUPLE
Name   Age of Children   M/F   Age(s) and gender of children
                                  with which you would
                                  like to work.
                                      Age(s)   Gender (M/F)

_____   _____

_____   _____

_____   _____

announcement referring to the "new member" who had voiced her need, was circled and a line drawn to the margin with these words, "John Ed, I was that new member. Thanks for a church that listens!" The church needs to hear the hurts and needs of people. Every congregation has a tremendous menu for ministry if it will only listen. Ministries based on needs are meaningful and exciting. Ministries designed to oil the machinery of the church become mundane, boring, and frustrating. Lay people today are eager to invest their lives in meaningful ministry—that is, ministry meeting needs.

Evaluation of Ministries

The church must constantly evaluate its process for determining needs to be sure that it is designing ministries, not to meet its own needs, but to meet the real needs of real people. It is easy for a congregation to become inwardly focused so that its ministry is just to keep the congregation alive. Its money, time, and effort are spent to serve the church rather than focusing on serving the needs of people. The needs that get the ministry attention must be the needs of people.

One of the problems with many congregations is that we do not know how to discontinue ministries that are no longer needed. I believe most congregations need a funeral service for activities they are continuing simply because they have always been around! So much of the money and energy of a congregation are wasted on ministries that might have had some meaning in the past, but serve no purpose in the present.

The cutting edge for ministry in the 1990s will be the ability of a congregation to listen to the needs of people, and then to design ministries to meet those needs. Every congregation has tremendous needs in its parish area. Every congregation has a strong cadre of lay people who have talents and can meet those needs. The task of the church is to put the laity in ministry at the point of the need of the people.

The Joel Committee at Frazer suggests that each ministry of the church be evaluated yearly by the Council on Ministries. One of the evaluating criteria is whether or not it meets the need for which it was designed. If it no longer meets that need, it will not be funded financially or staffed with volunteers. The other criterion for evaluating the ministry is whether or not it is a vehicle for implementing our priority of making disciples.

CHAPTER 7
DELINEATE STRENGTHS AND WEAKNESSES

The next step for the Joel Committee is to delineate the strengths and weaknesses of the congregation. I have a hunch that many congregations spend a lot of time, energy, and money trying to correct their weaknesses rather than utilizing well their strengths.

A good athletic team knows its strengths and uses them. A football team does not go into an important game trying to work on its weaknesses. That team has a plan designed around its strengths, and it utilizes these strengths to carry out the plan. Churches need to know what their strengths are and utilize them.

One of the instruments we have used at Frazer to work on this is a simple questionnaire distributed at a worship service that requests people to write down what they perceive as the three greatest strengths of Frazer and the three greatest weaknesses. We selected the worship service because this involves a good cross-section of people and includes members who have been a part of the congregation for a long time, as well as new members and visitors.

Music

We have discovered that one of our greatest strengths is music. We have taken that strength and put it to use. The more a strength is utilized, the stronger it becomes. Whatever we do well and often, we become better at doing.

Worship is the setting where more people are involved than at any other single event. If music is our strength, we decided to "run with our strength" and make music a larger part of our worship experience.

Each Sunday morning we have two places for special music in the worship service. Usually the choir presents two anthems, or occasionally a soloist or ensemble will sing. The choir also presents a call to worship, a call to sing, a chorus entitled "Surely the Presence of the Lord Is in This Place" before the morning prayer, and the ending of

Molotte's "Lord's Prayer" at the conclusion of the praying of the Lord's Prayer.

We also sing at least three hymns in each worship service. Because our worship services are geared to unchurched people, we always try to sing familiar hymns. We are very aware that if a person who hasn't attended in several years comes to a worship service, and doesn't recognize any of the hymns, that person feels as if he/she might be in the wrong place.

One of the basic principles of Frazer is the *participation* of all people. If people do not participate in singing the hymns, they are not likely to participate in serving in ministry during the week. The worship experience becomes a model of participation which most of our people will follow throughout the week.

Our music is people-related. Our choir has no paid members and no one has to audition to be a part of it. One of the principles at Frazer is that people participate. The Minister of Music would rather have 150 people singing a hymn than to have fifteen excellently trained musicians singing a difficult number that the congregation does not understand or relate to. Church music should be for the people.

I recently received a letter from a family in the Midwest who worship with us by television on the ACTS network each Sunday. The family was commenting on the meaningful music and wrote:

Dear Mr. Mathison,

We wanted to write and thank you for the very meaningful worship services we see on ACTS. We watch at 8:00 p.m. on Sunday nights. We especially want to commend the Music Ministry of Joe Pat Cox. It goes without saying that the music at Frazer, in toto, is gloriously magnificent, and absolutely without peer.

The truly unique feature of your music, however, is that it is programmed to reach the hearts of the Frazer Family. Most other Music Ministers present performances for their peers (i.e., other musicians) rather than for the edification of all the worshipers.

What we are saying is that even though we don't know anything about music, we love and are inspired by the music from The Frazer Methodist Hour.

Please continue to offer a Worship Service on television that relates to lay people!

The music ministry has become so strong that on fifth Sundays, four times a year, we have a "Fifth Sunday Service of Singing." The whole worship service centers around music. The choirs and special groups present six anthems or special numbers. Rather than a twenty-minute sermon, I preach about six two-minute sermons which introduce the music and connect it to the general theme of the worship experience. I usually give the background story of why a particular hymn was written; then we sing the hymn so that we might appreciate it more as we sing it in the future.

The fifth Sunday service of singing always closes with the entire congregation joining hands and singing together "The Lord's Prayer." It is truly a worshipful experience.

A strength gets stronger. If a good musician moves to town, he/she wants to be part of a congregation that has a good music program. The music program then becomes stronger because good musicians are a part of it.

Friendliness

Another strength noted at Frazer is friendliness. The first thing people look for when they attend a congregation for the first time is whether or not they perceive an atmosphere that is friendly. First-time visitors to a church are not as interested in the building, the choir, the preacher, or the surroundings—the most important factor is whether or not the people are friendly. Hospitality is critical for a congregation that wants to attract new people.

Based on the strength that our congregation is friendly, and the need for friendliness, we have a place in each worship service where people turn around and greet the people around them. I want to be sure that every person in worship shakes hands, touches somebody, speaks to someone, and is spoken to by someone.

Building on the strength of friendliness, we also decided to have parking lot greeters—a large group of volunteers who help in the parking lot by directing cars to parking spaces and greeting people as they arrive. It makes a good impression on a visitor to have a parking lot usher offer assistance—giving directions, helping with small children, sheltering under an umbrella, and in many other ways. It is important for this (often) first impression to be a positive, friendly one.

Leadership

One of the strengths that has been registered at Frazer is the leadership capability of lay people. Frazer is blessed with excellent lay leadership. One way we try to utilize this strength is to communicate to lay people that when they assume a place of leadership, they are truly given the freedom to lead. The church staff will not be "looking over their shoulder" to be sure they are capable of leading. There must be a high trust level between clergy and laity.

This does not mean that accountability is unimportant. Leaders have to have an accountability structure—but it should not be a prohibitive structure that stymies creativity. Good accountability structures promote rather than deny creativity!

The trust level between laity and clergy is indicated by how much the clergy need to know about what the laity are doing. Some pastors want to know everything every lay person is doing in order to "keep their finger on the situation." I often say, "If the pastor knows everything going on in the church, there is not enough going on!"

Administrative Board Responsibilities

We carried this a step further, to the leadership of the Administrative Board. I feel people should be elected to the Administrative Board to serve. When the nominating committee meets and lists the persons who should be nominated to serve on the Administrative Board, we send a letter to each of those persons and list some minimal qualifications for serving. We state that it is a high honor to serve on the Board, but it is also a responsibility. Each proposed Board member makes a commitment to certain minimal qualifications before being elected to the Administrative Board. Following is a copy of the letter we send to every person who is suggested for nomination. The signature of the proposed Board member on the letter indicates willingness to serve in these specific ways.

It is important for congregations to spend much more time on their strengths and less time on their weaknesses. This does not mean that we should overlook our weaknesses—it is simply an admission that most congregations do very little constructively with their weaknesses. A lot of weaknesses can be handled if we spend more time expanding our strengths.

Dear Frazer Family Leader,

The Nominating Committee would like to submit your name for nomination to the Administrative Board for *(year)*. This is perhaps the highest honor the congregation can bestow on you. All decisions of the congregation are accountable to the Administrative Board. Your leadership qualities and commitment have led us to submit your name.

This is a great privilege, but also a responsibility. Your name is being submitted, not only for the honor that comes to you, but for the service you can give to the congregation. The Nominating Committee has suggested the following *minimal* qualifications for each Board member.

1. Support Frazer Memorial with your prayers, presence, gifts, and service.
2. Attend the Board meetings. *If absent,* you will be expected *to call the Secretary* or *Board Chairman (phone no.)*.
3. Serve as a host/sponsor to a new member family to help them become involved in the church. New members will be assigned to Administrative Board members alphabetically.
4. Serve as a Captain or Co-Captain and with the follow-up of our In His Steps campaign.
5. Help visit some inactive members when assigned.

Our congregation has adopted the rotating system whereby no member serves more than three consecutive years on the Board. However, since all officials in the congregation are elected for one year only, a person must be nominated each of the three years. The Board usually meets about eight times a year.

Our Charge Conference for electing officials will be *(day of week)* night, *(date)*. The Nominating Committee requests that we be permitted to submit your name as an Administrative Board member. If you consent to having your name submitted, *please complete the attached slip and return it to the church by (date)* in the enclosed self-addressed envelope. Should you find it necessary to decline for some reason, we will understand and delete your name.

The Book of Discipline of The United Methodist Church, paragraph 253, states: "Members of the Administrative Board shall be persons of genuine Christian character who love the church, are morally disciplined, are loyal to the ethical standards The United Methodist Church sets forth in the Social Principles, and are competent to administer its affairs."

The service of our church can be greatly strengthened through your leadership.

For the Cause of causes,
/s/ John Ed Mathison,
Senior Minister

Form to be returned by prospective Board Member:
1. Support Frazer Memorial with your prayers, presence, gifts, and service.
2. Attend the Board meetings. *If absent, you will be expected to call the secretary or Board Chairman (phone no.).*
3. Serve as a host/sponsor to a new member family to help them become involved in the church.
4. Serve as a Captain or Co-Captain and with the follow-up of our In His Steps Campaign.
5. Help visit with some inactive members when assigned.

_____ I will be pleased to have my name submitted for nomination in *(year),* and will commit myself to the five minimal qualifications listed above, adopted by the Administrative Board.

_____ I request that I not be nominated for leadership at this time.

Signed _____

CHAPTER 8
DELEGATE THE MINISTRY

In the 1990s the effective congregation will be one that teaches and practices the priesthood of all believers. What the Protestant Reformation sought to overcome in eliminating the gulf between clergy and laity, the twentieth century church has recreated. People sense a distinct difference between lay persons and clergy persons.

Every Member in Ministry

The New Testament makes no distinction between laity and clergy. The ministry of the New Testament church was in the hands of the laity. The task of the church of the 1990s is to give the ministry back to the laity! Liberating the laity to do meaningful ministry is one of the greatest opportunities that lies before the church!

In today's world, people seem to use the number of associate ministers on a church staff as a measuring guide for the strength and effectiveness of a congregation. At Frazer, since we utilize laity for doing the ministry, and lay people are staff members, we don't have a large number of ordained ministers on the staff. I mentioned this to some lay people one day, almost apologetically, and one of them quickly replied, "Actually we have 6000 associate ministers because each of us is a minister!" That's good theology.

The Joel Committee at Frazer has given high priority to the development of a strategy that would allow lay people to become involved in meaningful ministry. After much prayerful consideration, it was felt that giving people an opportunity to volunteer for ministry was far more effective than trying to recruit them. The congregation decided to incorporate the financial program for seeking pledges into a program of total stewardship involving more than just money. Every person who joins The United Methodist Church makes a pledge to support the church by his or her prayers, presence, gifts, and service.

Taking this concept a step further, Frazer has now built its commitment program around these four aspects which touch on a complete commitment.

A Concept of Commitment

Each year in November, every member of Frazer is presented with a commitment card. On this card is a place to renew one's commitment in each of the four areas for the upcoming year. Much attention is given in worship, Sunday school, and in congregational publications to the importance of this time of commitment. We have called it our "In His Steps Campaign."

Each member of Frazer receives a commitment card (see sample below). Also please note that Discipleship Resources makes available a *Time and Talent Inventory* which covers many of the same areas of service (order no. E244T).

IN HIS STEPS
COMMITMENT CARD

After prayerful consideration I/we acknowledge our commitment to walk in the steps of Christ by:

1. Serving in His church as indicated below _____.
2. Praying for His church _____times per week.
3. Attending His church _____times per month.
4. Making the following financial FAITH INVESTMENT in His Church in 1991:

Operating Budget and Mortgage	Building Expansion	Early Debt Retirement
_____ per week	_____ per week	_____ per week
_____ per month	_____ per month	_____ per month
_____ other (specify)	_____ other (specify)	_____ other (specify)

Signed_____ Name_____

(Please print as your name/names will appear on the contribution evelope)

---

*THROUGH GOD'S HELP, I WILL COMMIT MYSELF TO DO HIS
WORK THROUGH FRAZER MEMORIAL UNITED METHODIST CHURCH
BY VOLUNTEERING FOR:*

ADMINISTRATIVE
Male   Female
( )   1 ( ) Office Volunteer
( )   2 ( ) Safety/Bus Committee
( )   3 ( ) Bus/Van Driver
( )   4 ( ) Calligraphy
( )   5 ( ) Computer Data Input
( )   6 ( ) Participation/Don Hill TV

AGE LEVEL MINISTRIES
Nursery Ministries
( )   8 ( ) Serve as Captain/Co-Captain
( )   9 ( ) Nursery 1x/mo 8:30
( )   10 ( ) Nursery 1x/mo 9:40
( )   11 ( ) Nursery 1x/mo 11:00
( )   12 ( ) Nursery 1x/mo 6:30 p.m.
( )   13 ( ) Teach 2-yr. Sun. School
( )   14 ( ) Music Ministry 1x/mo 9:40
( )   15 ( ) Visit New Mothers/Cradle Roll
( )   16 ( ) Deliver Rose/Bibles/Yard Signs
( )   17 ( ) Friends for Life

Children's Ministries
( )   18 ( ) Teach Sunday School
( )   19 ( ) Substitute in Sun. School
( )   20 ( ) Help/Child. Church-Preschool
( )   21 ( ) Help/Child. Church-Elem.
( )   22 ( ) Assist in Handicapped Class
( )   23 ( ) Help in High Flyers
( )   24 ( ) Vacation Bible School
( )   25 ( ) Children's Choir-Dir/Helper
( )   26 ( ) Children's Choir Pianist
( )   27 ( ) Help in Day Camp (local)
( )   28 ( ) Help in Elem. Camp-Blue Lake

Youth Ministries
( )   29 ( ) Teach in Sunday School
( )   30 ( ) Assist in Sunday School
( )   31 ( ) Christmas Tree Sales
( )   32 ( ) Serve UMYF Snack Suppers
( )   33 ( ) Help w/Work Project
( )   34 ( ) Transportation for Work Project
( )   35 ( ) Have Afterglow on Sun. night
( )   36 ( ) Covenant Group Leader
( )   37 ( ) Jr. High Wed. Bible Study
( )   38 ( ) Youth Choir Parent Team

College Ministries
( )   39 ( ) Teach Sunday School
( )   40 ( ) Lead Small Group Bible Study
( )   41 ( ) Disciple One Student
( )   42 ( ) Host Late Night Fellowship
( )   43 ( ) Assist-Campus Evangelism
( )   44 ( ) Adopt one out-of-town Student
( )   45 ( ) Coach Intramural Sports
( )   46 ( ) Host Retreat (Lake/Beach house)

Single Adult Ministries
( )   47 ( ) Children's Weekday Program
( )   48 ( ) Support/Discipleship Groups
( )   49 ( ) Substitute Teach

Adult Ministries
( )   50 ( ) Teach Sunday School
( )   51 ( ) Easter Egg Hunt
( )   52 ( ) Bethel Series Secretary
( )   53 ( ) One-on-One Tutoring

Older Adult Ministries
( )   54 ( ) Transport-3rd and 4th Thurs.
( )   55 ( ) Teach Crafts—4th Thurs.
( )   56 ( ) Help w/Friends-3rd Thurs.
( )   57 ( ) Help w/4th Thursday
( )   58 ( ) Coordinate Trips

Family Ministries
( )   59 ( ) Spring Festival
( )   60 ( ) Fall Festival
( )   61 ( ) Special Events

Church and Society
( )   62 ( ) Blood Donor
( )   63 ( ) Blood Drive Worker
( )   64 ( ) Prison Ministry
( )   65 ( ) Substance Abuse Ministry
( )   66 ( ) Victims Support Ministry
( )   67 ( ) Family Issues/Concerns

Congregational Care
( )   68 ( ) Lay Minister Program
( )   69 ( ) Hospital Ministry
( )   70 ( ) Shut-In Ministry
( )   71 ( ) Nursing Home Ministry
( )   72 ( ) Grief Crisis Support
( )   73 ( ) Flower Del. (Hospitals)
( )   74 ( ) PAWS (Pets Are Working Saints)
( )   75 ( ) Alzheimer's Disease Ministry
( )   76 ( ) Transportation-Elderly Appts.

Education
( )   77 ( ) Sunday School Secretary-8:15
( )   78 ( ) Sunday School Secretary-9:30
( )   79 ( ) Sunday School Secretary-11:00

Ethic Minority
( )   81 ( ) Special Projects
( )   82 ( ) Adult Literacy

Evangelism
( )   83 ( ) Neighborhood Visitation
( )   84 ( ) Attendance Data Entry
( )   85 ( ) Telephone Committee
( )   86 ( ) New Member Photography

Food Service
( )   87 ( ) Sun. Breakfast 1x/mo.
( )   88 ( ) Snack Supper 1x/mo.

( ) 89 ( ) Wed. Night Supper 1x/mo.
( ) 90 ( ) Noon Salad Luncheon
( ) 91 ( ) 4th Thursday/Friends
( ) 92 ( ) Hospitality

Health and Welfare
( ) 93 ( ) Selma Children's Home
( ) 94 ( ) Angel Tree Christmas Program

Leisure Ministries
( ) 95 ( ) Coach Ladies' Softball
( ) 96 ( ) Coach Men's Softball
( ) 97 ( ) Coach Youth Softball
( ) 98 ( ) Coach Men's Basketball
( ) 99 ( ) Coach Youth Basketball
( ) 100 ( ) Lead Exercise Program
( ) 101 ( ) Boy Scouts
( ) 102 ( ) Cub Scouts
( ) 103 ( ) Girl Scouts

Missions—In Christ Way
( ) 104 ( ) Spiritual Follow-Up
( ) 105 ( ) Professional/Work Skills
( ) 106 ( ) Financial Counseling
( ) 107 ( ) Christian Job Exchange
( ) 108 ( ) Food Pantry
( ) 109 ( ) Clothes Closet

Missions—Local
( ) 110 ( ) Meals on Wheels
( ) 111 ( ) S.T.E.P.
( ) 112 ( ) Bell Street-Sun. School
( ) 113 ( ) Bell Street V.B.S.
( ) 114 ( ) Bell Street—Tutor

Missions—World and National
( ) 115 ( ) World and National Outreach
( ) 116 ( ) Serve on a Work Team
( ) 117 ( ) Serve on a Medical Team
( ) 118 ( ) Pray for Missionary
( ) 119 ( ) Correspond with Missionary
( ) 120 ( ) House Missionaries
( ) 121 ( ) $10 Club

Music
( ) 122 ( ) Adult Choir-Morning
( ) 123 ( ) Adult Choir-Evening
( ) 124 ( ) Older Adult Choir
( ) 125 ( ) Instrument Ensembles
( ) 126 ( ) Pianist

Newspaper Ministry
( ) 127 ( ) Writers
( ) 128 ( ) Proofreaders
( ) 129 ( ) Design and Layout
( ) 130 ( ) Still Photography
( ) 131 ( ) Data Input

Prayer Ministry
( ) 132 ( ) "Upper Room" Prayer
( ) 133 ( ) Prayer and Fasting

Religious Drama
( ) 134 ( ) Acting/Directing
( ) 135 ( ) Costumes
( ) 136 ( ) Make-Up
( ) 137 ( ) Spotlight
( ) 138 ( ) Scenery

Stewardship
( ) 139 ( ) Lay Reader 8:15
( ) 140 ( ) Lay Reader 9:30
( ) 141 ( ) Lay Reader 11:00
( ) 142 ( ) New Member Orientation
( ) 143 ( ) New Member Packets
( ) 144 ( ) Lay Involvement Coordination

United Methdist Women
( ) 145 ( ) Member UMW Circle
( ) 146 ( ) Interested in UMW Circle

United Methodist Men
( ) 147 ( ) Interested in UMM

Worship
( ) 148 ( ) Sanctuary Usher 1x/mo 8:15
( ) 149 ( ) Sanctuary Usher 1x/mo 9:30
( ) 150 ( ) Sanctuary Usher 1x/mo 11:00
( ) 151 ( ) Sanctuary Usher 1x/mo 7:00 pm
( ) 152 ( ) Parking Usher 1x/mo
( ) 153 ( ) Communion Usher/Server 8:15
( ) 154 ( ) Communion Usher/Server 9:30
( ) 155 ( ) Communion Usher/Server 11:00
( ) 156 ( ) Communion Preparation
( ) 157 ( ) Greeter 1x/mo 8:15
( ) 158 ( ) Greeter 1x/mo 9:30
( ) 159 ( ) Greeter 1x/mo 11:00
( ) 160 ( ) Count Attendance
( ) 161 ( ) Acolyte Coordinator

Worship Support Area
( ) 162 ( ) Special Decorations
( ) 163 ( ) Sanctuary Care
( ) 164 ( ) Altar Care

Miscellaneous
( ) 165 ( ) Wherever the Church Needs Me
( ) 166 ( ) Other (Specify)

_____

Name _____

Address _____

Telephone (_____)_____

Each member of Frazer receives this card and is invited to return it on Commitment Sunday. On that day different people share what Christ is doing in their lives through Frazer and where they are serving. At the close of the worship service, each member comes forward and places his/her commitment card on the altar. People who are not present that Sunday morning are involved in a follow-up campaign that week. The ministry is designed to receive a card from every member concerning their commitment of prayers, presence, gifts, and service.

The first area of commitment on the card is praying for the church. Members are asked to write down the number of times they will pray for the Frazer congregation in the coming year. Prayer can be such a generalized feeling that people never become specific about praying. Each member is expected to pray for the congregation each day.

Naturally, people have different levels of commitment to the ministry of prayer. While any member can pray for the church each day, some members may want to do more. On the commitment card there is a full section of ministry opportunities under the general heading of Prayer Ministry. People can commit themselves to one hour a week praying for specific prayer requests at the church building. People can also volunteer to be a part of the Prayer and Fasting Ministry. The card provides a specific, intentional opportunity for prayer.

The next section of the card involves a commitment to attend worship. Each member will make a commitment concerning how many times that member will attend in the upcoming year. Making a commitment in November for the following year helps people see the importance of the congregation as it gathers to celebrate in worship each Sunday.

In January 1990, an extreme cold front moved through Montgomery on Sunday morning. The temperature was down in the low teens. When I arrived at church early that Sunday morning, I saw one of our oldest members present. I was surprised that she came out on a Sunday when the weather was so bitter. My first comment to her was appreciation for her being there. Then I told her I was a little surprised that she had decided to come in spite of the weather. She looked at me quickly and said, "John Ed, I didn't decide to come to church this morning, I decided last November when I made a commitment to be here fifty Sundays this year. If I had waited until today to decide, I probably wouldn't have come. I had already made that decision." Wow!

The intent of this ministry came home to me in concrete form through that beautiful lady. The process of making a commitment early helps later commitments come more easily.

The third area of commitment involves a financial commitment. We stress the importance of tithing and teach this as a standard that God expects for the church. We have a lot of people witness to the importance of tithing in their Christian experience. Each member is expected to make a financial commitment for the upcoming year.

The Commitment Card contains three different areas for financial commitments: (1) The Operating Budget includes all of the regular, ongoing expenses of the local church; (2) the Building Fund is an opportunity to give to future facility needs; (3) the Early Debt Retirement Fund is designed to eliminate the indebtedness of the congregation so that the money that has been used to pay interest can be used for more creative ministries. In 1990 the Frazer Family pledged $3.7 million to the Operating Budget, $400,000 to future building, and $370,000 to debt retirement. Making a commitment for the coming year helps the church do its financial planning. It also helps individuals establish habits of good stewardship.

The last area on the commitment card concerns the place for service. Frazer operates on the concept of volunteerism. The card lists 166 different ministries for which members may volunteer to serve. A person may volunteer in more than one area.

One of the exciting features of the commitment card in the area of service is the last section which reads "Other." Here people are invited to suggest a ministry or to volunteer their service in an area in which the church might not be presently involved. Many of the new ministries at Frazer have been developed from this section of the card where people have volunteered. This is an excellent place for the church to "listen" to the perceived needs and recognized gifts of lay people.

One exciting ministry that grew out of this area is our prison ministry. A member simply indicated some experience in prison ministry and a desire to go to the prisons to minister. One week, we announced in the worship bulletin the opportunity for developing a prison ministry and asked for volunteers. Many people volunteered and the prison ministry was begun. Today we have about 100 people involved in a prison ministry in eight different prisons in our area.

Another exciting ministry that came out of this was the PAWS Ministry. PAWS is an acronym for *Pets Are Working Saints*. A woman indicated that many older adults and people with mental and physical handicaps relate extremely well to pets. She had some expertise in training pets and wanted to see if pets might be used to minister to these persons.

This idea for ministry was quite different from anything we had tried before, but it was given a chance. A lot of people volunteered. Today there are over 100 people involved in this ministry and over seventy pets, including dogs, cats, birds, rabbits, etc., that have passed the temperament test and have been trained to participate in this ministry.

The PAWS ministry has had a tremendous influence in the city of Montgomery with older adults and persons with handicapping conditions. The prison ministry also is utilizing the PAWS ministry with some of the inmates on death row. Some of these inmates were extremely hardened and refused to talk to any person. The PAWS ministry came to them with some pets, the prisoners became interested in the pets, and that opened a door for meaningful conversation and ministry in their lives!

It is important to emphasize that this card is not an "interest survey" or "talent search"—it is a commitment card. People are expected to pray, attend, give, and serve as they indicate on this card. It is a *commitment* card.

This card is a commitment for one year only. A lot of people are afraid to accept a responsibility in the church, because they are afraid they might have that responsibility for many years in the future. Every ministry of service concludes at the end of the year. The term of commitment has a definite ending point. A person may volunteer for the same area the next year, but this year's commitment is only for this year.

This one-year commitment frees people up to take a chance and volunteer for something for which they might not be completely certain. The risk factor is not so great if people know from the beginning that they will be allowed to change areas of ministry next year.

Burnout

An important aspect of the one-year commitment based on volunteering is the impact on "burnout." Much has been written lately about lay people who "burn out" because they have so many responsibilities for such a long time. The "In His Steps Campaign" allows people to select a place to serve where they feel God's calling. Members have a sense of being gifted for the ministry, and have a one-year commitment timeline. If the sense of calling is not reinforced during the year, or if the need for ministry changes, or if the lay person discovers a stronger sense of calling in another ministry, there is opportunity to move on in ministry. This is an excellent remedy for burnout.

The effectiveness of this approach at Frazer is well illustrated by an experience we had. A local newspaper called for an appointment to interview me. The paper was running a special series on volunteer "burnout." As I talked to the reporter, it dawned on me that I could not name one lay person at Frazer who had complained of "burnout." I invited the reporter to talk with other staff persons, and not one of them could name a person who "burned out." Our conclusion was that people were so excited about the ministry to which God had called them, and to which they had volunteered, that the conditions for burnout simply did not exist at Frazer.

Volunteerism

Volunteering is important. There is a ministry niche for every person. Every new member at Frazer is told that he/she is expected to become involved in a ministry. When people join the congregation, they are immediately invited to attend a new member orientation class at which time they receive a commitment card. The function of the membership orientation class is to share information about the various ministries and to encourage people to get involved immediately. As people join during the year, they are immediately trained and incorporated into these ministries.

At Frazer we have also discovered a very important principle: Every person who volunteers for a ministry must be given an opportunity to serve in that ministry. A lot of congregations ask people to volunteer but never follow up on responses. If you say volunteering is important, and do not follow up on the person who has volunteered, then the program will have no credibility in subsequent years.

We do all the follow-up on volunteers through staff persons and lay persons. Each area of ministry is under the direction of a staff person and a lay person. Persons who have volunteered in a specific area will be contacted by the staff person and the lay person responsible for that area, thanking them for volunteering and giving them information about the training session. Accountability for follow-up is essential!

Training is essential. Everyone needs to know how the church expects them to do the particular ministry for which they volunteered. The training process also gives credibility to the ministry, gives volunteers confidence in their ministry area, and opens the door for creative and innovative ideas for the ministry. Because training of volunteers is a high priority, Frazer's church year for service operates from February 1 to January 31 in order to utilize the month of January for training. The financial year is the calendar year. Commitment cards are returned in November. Due to all the activities involved during the Christmas season, we devote the entire month of January to training volunteers. Every volunteer attends a training session in January before assuming responsibility for a ministry function in February.

One of the important aspects of volunteerism is that it gives a great responsibility to lay people. If the church is really going to turn ministry functions over to lay people, it should also trust the lay people to know best where they can serve. Staff persons are never smart enough to be able to determine where people should be recruited to serve. The volunteer concept says that individual members should prayerfully consider the opportunities and let God lead them to the place(s) where they ought to serve. God doesn't make mistakes! The Spirit of God places people in the right place!

The volunteer concept also gives ownership of ministry to lay persons. When lay persons volunteer for ministry rather than being recruited for it, they have ownership of that decision. When lay persons prayerfully consider their own gifts and match them to an area of ministry, feeling God leading them to this service, they have ownership of the decision and commitment to the ministry.

I try to reinforce the whole concept of volunteering in worship services and in the various ministries of the church. At Frazer we invite people to witness in the worship service concerning how and where they are serving, and why they felt God was leading them to serve in a particular area. Oftentimes during the part of a worship service where people greet each other, I suggest they turn to the people around them and share information about where they are serving in the life of the church. This helps reinforce the importance of every member's participation in ministry.

Frazer has a basic stance that God leads people to volunteer for the right places to serve. We say that if no one volunteers for a particular ministry, then God is not calling us to that ministry! If no one volunteers, we drop the ministry! This makes the prayerful consideration for volunteering extremely important.

The volunteering concept also has a lot of financial implications. A prime example is the Food Service Ministry at Frazer which, in 1990, served an average of 1800 meals a week! All of this was done through the over 600 food service volunteers. One woman is paid part-time as a staff member to coordinate the volunteers, and two part-time helpers assist her in planning the menus, buying the food, etc. The rest is done by volunteers. One of the areas to volunteer for service is in helping with cooking and serving the various meals. If volunteers are available, meals are prepared and served. If no one volunteers for specific meals, we won't go out and hire people to cook and serve those meals.

Another dramatic illustration of the power of volunteerism is the Television Ministry. Frazer's morning worship service is shown live on the most powerful VHF television station in the state of Alabama. It is also played, a week delayed, on the ACTS Network, which has a potential viewing audience of several million people. The evening worship service is televised locally. Dr. Don Hill of the Frazer Counseling Center has a weekly television program in the Montgomery area. The entire Television Ministry is carried out by unpaid volunteers. There are over eighty people who operate the cameras, produce the programs, etc.

The volunteer concept gives lay people the opportunity to evaluate their own gifts and graces. The congregation gives a menu of ministries to which God is calling, and then gives people the opportunity to volunteer for the place God is leading them to serve. This places the ministry in the hands of the laity—where the Bible teaches it should be.

Follow-Up of Visitors

The Joel Committee's heavy emphasis on delegating the ministry and utilizing lay people is well illustrated in the specific ways in which the Frazer family reaches out to new people and follows up on visitors. The emphasis on the ministry of the laity, and the effectiveness of the volunteer concept, are the foundations of invitation and visitation follow-up.

I stated earlier that our priority at Frazer is to make disciples. At Frazer, we want to be reaching out to new people all the time, but our basic concept is that *people bring people.* Our work area on evangelism has decided not to go into neighborhoods door by door in order to invite people to church. Such visits often make people feel awkward or even invaded. Cold calls are extremely difficult. By contrast, our emphasis at Frazer is to encourage every member of the congregation to invite people to come to worship. Then, when a follow-up visit is made—usually by a lay person to a lay person—the visitor is far more receptive to such a visit than to a "cold" call.

This also places the emphasis on the participation of the entire congregation in the work of evangelism by inviting people. We interview every person who joins Frazer, and have discovered that 86 percent of the people visit because a friend invited them. Even though we have tremendous exposure through television and radio, tremendous ministries with age-level groups, excellent accessibility and visibility, the number one reason people come is because people bring people. That is the foundation of our evangelism outreach.

Let me walk through the specifics the work area on evangelism has utilized in follow-up. Let me also emphasize that this changes from year to year as the personality of the people involved and the cultural and social situations dictate.

On Sunday morning, as a part of the worship service, every worshiper registers his/her attendance on a standard registration pad (available in sets of 20 pads from Discipleship Resources, order no. A003P). This is much more effective than having visitors raise their hands or stand up. Most visitors do not want to be formally recognized or made to stand out in a crowd. Both members and visitors place their names and other requested information on the registration pad on Sunday morning.

On Sunday afternoon a group of people who have volunteered in the area of worship attendance registration in evangelism meet and go through the sheets containing the names of the worshipers. For several years we kept a membership file manually, but now we do it both manually and by computer. Some people say it would require too much time to record the attendance of all the worshipers. We have discovered that our volunteers can register the attendance of 4000 worshipers in about two hours on Sunday afternoon!

If a man visits Frazer for the first time on Sunday morning and registers his attendance, his name then goes onto the computer as a visitor. The address and any information he supplies is recorded on the data sheet. On Monday morning all the visitors are sorted by neighborhoods, as we do our visitation by neighborhoods. We have families in each neighborhood who have volunteered to visit and have been trained to visit, so visiting by neighborhoods allows the volunteers to visit effectively in a familiar area.

One of the questions usually raised is whether or not visitors should make appointments before they go for a visit. Our visitors are trained to do this however they feel most comfortable. Most of our visitors do not make appointments, because we have discovered that people have a tendency to put visitors off for several days.

It is important to visit people immediately after they have visited the congregation. The best time is on Sunday afternoon, or on Monday or Tuesday night. We tell our visitors that if they cannot make the visit by Wednesday, we prefer to give the name to someone else to visit. There is a definite relationship between the timeliness of the visit and the effectiveness of the results from the visit. Visits should be made within three days.

I recently attended a meeting where a man from another congregation told me that, two nights earlier, he was visiting a couple who had joined Frazer. When I inquired about his friendship with them, he quickly said that he was visiting them on church business because he was on his congregation's evangelism committee. He explained that they had visited his congregation about five Sundays ago. He had received their name for visitation, but had been so busy, he only found the time that week for the visit. His visit was a little late—they had already joined Frazer.

Out of curiosity, I checked to see when the couple visited Frazer. They actually had visited the other congregation first, but the laity of

Frazer had followed up with a visit within thirty-six hours, had contacted them through a Sunday school class, and had brought them to the family night dinner on the Wednesday after they visited on Sunday!

To continue with the description of our process, on Monday afternoon the Minister of Evangelism goes through the visitors' names and assigns each of them to a neighborhood visitor. The neighborhood visitor is then contacted by phone or comes by the church Monday afternoon and picks up a duplicate card for visitation. Those who visit have duplicate cards on which they place the visitor information. The duplicate card is the accountability system. The neighborhood visitor has to report back to the church office the date and results of the visit. Always have an accountability system in visitation. Never give out slips and hope people will return them with the information on the completed visit. Accountability is essential!

Most people will stop and make the visit on their way home from work. If that is not a convenient time, they can come back in an hour or so. Oftentimes the first contact or visit is of a very casual nature where people simply want information about the church. The evangelism visitor is trained to be sensitive—to relate to the person at the level at which the person indicates an interest.

One of the advantages of neighborhood visitation is that if the person joins the church, the visitor who called on that person lives in the same neighborhood and will have some social contact with that person. This neighborhood friendship will also be helpful in assimilating that person into the congregation.

The evangelism visitor may need to make a follow-up visit or indicate that someone else should visit the person. The evangelism committee responds at the level of need of the person who has been visited.

It is important to have lay people make the initial contact: People are far more responsive to a lay visitor than to a staff person. Lay people are also more effective at making the visit because they can relate more effectively to the visitor.

Assimilation of New Members

Let me also walk through the process of how people are assimilated into the life of the congregation at Frazer when they join. (You will remember this was one of the specific recommendations of the Joel

Committee in 1980.) We are constantly evaluating and revising the manner in which people are assimilated into the life of Frazer.

We have a basic emphasis in two areas for new members—to get them involved in a small group, and to get them involved in a function of ministry. Studies show that when people join a congregation, if within six months they are not involved in a small group or function of ministry, 50 percent of them become inactive. Therefore, it is essential to get people involved immediately.

When people join the church on Sunday morning, they receive a letter from the pastor the following week welcoming them as new members to the Frazer family. They also receive a visit from a member of the Stewardship Committee who brings them a packet of material providing basic information about the church. Also, a new member is immediately assigned to an Administrative Board member. You will remember that each Administrative Board member has agreed to serve as a sponsor of a new member. The Administrative Board member has been trained to visit that new member, to answer questions about the church, and to bring the new person(s) to a New Member Orientation Class.

The function of the New Member Orientation each month is to get the new member involved immediately in a small group and in a function of ministry. At the New Member Orientation the commitment card is explained and new members are given an opportunity to complete one, beginning the process of getting involved in a small group and in a function of ministry.

The function of the Administrative Board member is to sponsor that new member for a few months until he/she becomes involved in the ministry of the church. When people become actively involved they do not become a problem as an inactive. The best way to eliminate inactives is the preventive measure of implementing a ministry of assimilation for new members!

The visitation of prospective members and the assimilation of new members are carried out by lay people who have volunteered for these ministries. The concept is to have lay people giving leadership to lay people to get them involved.

One of the goals we set is to have no more than 15 percent of the congregation's membership inactive. We consider any person who has missed six consecutive Sundays as inactive. This is a goal we set and report at the staff meetings and the Council on Ministries. This is one of those diagnostic indications of potential problems if the inactive percentage starts to increase. For the year 1990 we were able to reach our goal, as we maintained an inactive list of only 13 percent! (In computing our percentage, we eliminate the members who have moved away, and those who are shut-in, since they cannot be in worship.)

The best people for inviting other people to come to church are the newest members. When new members join the church and become actively involved in a meaningful ministry, those members become excited and want to invite their friends. The best inviters are those who have joined, are enthusiastic, and want to tell their friends about it.

Another important feature of getting people involved is that people who are actively involved have little time to grumble or cause dissension. My father used to say, "You cannot row the boat and rock it at the same time." A bee cannot sting and give honey at the same time. Most people in the church who cause the most problems are those who are on the periphery and are not serving in some meaningful way. By delegating the ministries of the congregation to the people of the congregation, you not only follow the positive biblical model of the church in action, you also avoid a great many problems that plague the institutional church.

CHAPTER 9
DESIGN EXCITING, MEANINGFUL WORSHIP

Worship is the "front porch" of the church. More people attend worship than any other function of ministry. Therefore, worship needs to be exciting and meaningful.

Evaluate the Worship Experience

The work area on worship at Frazer distributed a survey asking people's opinions about the most important elements of worship and which parts of the worship service were least meaningful to them. We wanted to listen to what the people who worshiped were saying.

The first expectation people had for worship was that it should be lively and celebrative. It should be designed so that people can participate in worship. Worship is not intended to be a spectator sport. It is for participation by all of the people. If people do not participate in worship, they are not likely to participate in serving throughout the week!

It was interesting to note that respondents said the pastoral prayer was one of the least effective parts of the worship experience. People today are not accustomed to sitting with their eyes closed for a long period of time. Visual experiences prompt a more favorable response. People surveyed also said they had a hard time determining whether the pastor was speaking to God, or speaking to them, or trying to say something nice for the people to hear, or something nice for God to hear. All of them agreed that the pastoral prayer should be limited to two minutes.

It was also felt that some of the responses in the order of worship each Sunday become redundant and tend to lose their meaning. This also was felt to be true of regularly recited material (creeds, etc.). Currently, the only unison recitation each Sunday is The Lord's Prayer. The creed and some of the responses are included at various times, but not on a regular basis.

Let the People Participate!

The survey indicated it was very important that worshipers be able to participate in the singing of the hymns. Having about 750 visitors each Sunday, we realized that it is important to design the worship service so a person who has not been in church for several years will feel that some hymn is at least familiar. For this reason, as mentioned above, we intentionally place at least one hymn in each order of worship that most people have heard and know.

The actual singing of the hymns is also very important. This is one point in the service where the people enjoy participating. Having a lot of people singing and participating in the music is one way to make a service alive and exciting.

Music is a vital part of worship. Many churches miss the important contribution that music can make because worship is designed around anthems and featured performers rather than full congregational participation. In many churches music is for the musicians, not the people. Many choir anthems are out of touch with where the congregation is. Music has to be "for the heart as well as for art."

Along with music, we recognize other ways to enhance participation. At most worship services we invite a lay person to participate by giving a three-minute witness. This visibly shows the importance of lay participation and shows that lay people are experiencing God's grace in many different ways. This also gives lay people permission to share their faith in everyday situations.

We also encourage lay persons to read the scripture. Also the scripture appears in the worship bulletin so that every person can follow along. This is another point at which every worshiper can participate. If a person doesn't sing well and doesn't participate in the hymns, at least that person can participate in reading together the scripture.

Yet another dimension of participation has to do with the *tone* of worship. Worship should be good news. Most people come to worship looking for some direction for their life. Worship should focus on the immense possibilities God provides for every person if we will submit ourselves to God's will. This doesn't mean that worship needs to portray a "pie in the sky" theology or a "populist" approach. Sin must certainly be recognized and identified, but the possibility of victory over sin is the good news that worship needs to communicate.

Sermon Outline

Another path to participation is the use of a sermon outline with the Sunday bulletin. I provide a sermon outline for the congregation each Sunday (see sample below). An outline provides worshipers a place to make notes and follow the sermon. I also list Bible verses on the outline so that people can go home during the week and look up additional passages of scripture. I don't always cover all the passages on the outline during the sermon, but it helps people who can't write down all the biblical references.

Sample Sermon Outline

THERE'S SOMETHING ABOUT THAT NAME

Philippians 2:9-11

I. PREEMINENCE "name above every name" v. 9

Matt. 1:21
John 20:31
Acts 4:12

II. POWER "every knee shall bow" v. 10

1 Sam. 17:45
Acts 4:7, 10
John 14:13, 14; 15:16; 16:23

III. PROCLAMATION "every tongue confess" v. 11

Acts 4:18-20
Acts 5:33-41
Matt. 28:19, 20

Dr. John Ed Mathison
Date

I have also discovered that many people use the sermon outline as a source for study during the week. Some families use it for family devotions during the week so they can reflect on the morning worship experience. One of the obvious drawbacks to this for the preacher is that you can't use the sermon again!

The back of the sermon outline lists a prayer request for each day of the upcoming week. This gives the whole congregation a central focus for prayer each day and helps build a sense of togetherness in the congregation. Each person feels part of a larger cause, as that person joins others in a daily unified prayer request.

Indigenous Worship

The worship service must be indigenous. It must minister to the people participating and motivate them to service. It should be constantly evaluated by clergy and laity to be sure it is a celebration of the risen Lord and meets the need of those participating.

There is much discussion today about how formal a worship service should be. I would emphasize that the tone or structure is not as important as what the service communicates to those who are participating in it. The worship service must fit the personalities of the pastor and the people. It must be authentic.

Some pastors wear robes; some do not. I wore a robe until we began having three morning worship services. The robe was extremely hot, and I started having some throat problems. For practical reasons (and my doctor's advice) I stopped wearing the robe. I also discovered that most unchurched people in the South felt more comfortable in a worship setting without the use of robes. Each pastor and congregation has to make decisions about how formal or informal the worship service should be. The point is that the result should be a steppingstone and not a stumbling block for the worshipers.

Evening worship is also important at Frazer. We have discovered that many people work on Sunday mornings, or have other activities that make it imposible for them to attend a morning service of worship. Our evening service of worship is very informal and averages about 700 in attendance. Again, we focus on a lot of music and participation by the laity.

By this point, you will have noticed a repeating theme in several of the preceding chapters. We have encouraged involving lay people in planning. We have emphasized the importance of volunteerism and delegating ministry. And now, in order to achieve exciting and meaningful worship, we have underlined the value of participation. Someone may say that a worship service is participatory regardless of how "exciting" or "meaningful" it is. After all, even in a dull and boring service, the people are there. But the kind of participation that causes a congregation to grow is not just a matter of being there physically. It is a matter of being involved emotionally during the service and actively during the week. For that to happen, your worship service must be exciting and meaningful to those who participate.

CHAPTER 10
DEVELOP STAFF

First Corinthians 12 provides an excellent biblical basis for staff relationships. In this chapter the apostle Paul uses the human body as an analogy for what God expects the church to be. The human body is a unity of various parts with specific functions. Each part of the body functions to give unity to the body. Each part of the body has an individual contribution to make to the overall well-being and wholeness of the body.

Paul writes about the ears and eyes, and how each of them performs a specific function. The eye cannot hear and the ear cannot see. Each has a specific function that it is to perform, and it should not consider itself more important than the function offered by the other member. He also writes about the hands and the feet. Each serves a very specific and important function. The body is handicapped when some of its parts are not functioning properly. The unique contribution of the feet is as essential as the unique contribution of the hands.

The purpose of each of these parts of the body, according to Paul, is to contribute to the unity of the body. Each works together for the mutual good of the whole body. If certain parts of the body try to operate independently of the other parts, confusion and illness will result. The human body moves best when each of the individual parts functions appropriately. If my feet decide to go in one direction, and my hands decide to go in another direction, then I will fall flat on my face. Many church staffs and congregations find themselves flat on their faces because the individual parts of the body are trying to go in opposite directions.

Specialized Rather Than Generalized Responsibilities

I believe a church staff should focus on the concept of specialized rather than generalized responsibilities. Ordained pastors are trained to be generalists. We have to be able to handle a multitude of ministries in the church. We have to lead worship, do organizational planning with the Council on Ministries, counsel people, be responsible for the financial accountability, direct the educational program, etc. We are trained to be generalists.

I would submit that a church staff should be built on specialized rather than generalized responsibilities. This is true even of small congregations where the "staff" includes only one ordained person working with a group of lay volunteers. If all the leaders of a congregation are generalists, then all are doing a little of the same thing, and many things begin to "fall through the cracks."

Specific responsibilities tend to deploy the gifts of individuals in the best manner and to give better accountability for the stewardship of ministries. Most staff people are not multi-talented, but every staff person has strengths in one or two specialized ministries. Building a church staff should give each person an opportunity to utilize his or her special gifts in a specific area of responsibility.

The same concept holds true for lay people as well as for ordained people—people really enjoy and find meaning in discovering and serving in their areas of expertise. Most of the energy of staff people—lay or clergy—should be focused in areas of expertise, not in generalized responsibilities for which they have very little talent or interest.

At Frazer, one of the examples of specialized ministry is our approach to education. We do not have an ordained Christian education director. Rather we have many part-time and full-time staff members with specific responsibilities. Very seldom do you find someone who can be an expert in nursery ministry, youth ministry, and older adult ministry!

We divide our education responsibilities into age-level departments. We have a part-time person who is responsible for nursery ministry. She has another part-time person working with her. Her only responsibility is nursery. She doesn't worry about the program for youth, or whether or not there is going to be a teacher in the children's division. Her responsibility is to minister to the families and children in the nursery area.

This woman's specific ministry goes far beyond caring for babies on Sunday morning. It is a full ministry which involves about 600 volunteers. A family in the maternity ward of the hospital receives a visit from someone in the nursery ministry. When the family brings their newborn home, they will find a large attractive sign in the front yard announcing the arrival of the child with the words, "Another member of the Frazer family lives here." Everybody in the neighborhood sees the sign.

A couple of weeks later, a nursery ministry representative will invite the parents to come to the church to see the specific room in which their baby will be cared for when they bring it to church. They fill out a lengthy questionnaire including such information as how and when the baby is fed, etc.

When the family arrives on the first Sunday, they see a picture of the baby on the bulletin board as one of the Frazer family's newest members. Later someone in the nursery ministry takes that picture, makes it into a Christmas ornament, and gives it to the family so one of the baby's first Christmas gifts is from the church family!

There are many other facets of this ministry, but it is a ministry to adults and babies. Studies show that the most important room in the church is the nursery. Parents are more concerned about the cleanliness, appealing decor, and staffing of the nursery than of any other room in the church. For growing congregations, a strong, solid nursery ministry is important.

Another illustration of specialized rather than generalized ministries at Frazer are the age-level ministries. In the children's ministry area we have one part-time director and three part-time assistants working together. We have a full-time person working with youth, a full-time person with singles, a full-time person with college students, a part-time person in young adult ministry, and a part-time person in older adult ministry. Each of these is a specialist in his/her area.

Part-Time Staff

The best way to facilitate specialized responsibilities is to consider the concept of part-time staff persons. Sixty-five percent of the staff at Frazer is part-time. With the exception of the appointed senior pastor, every staff position began as a part-time staff responsibility!

This allows a congregation to maximize the concept of specialized ministry by giving people an opportunity to serve in a specific way. There are a lot of people who are already involved in a vocation who might also serve in a part-time capacity on staff and fulfill a vocational calling. Frazer has three persons serving part-time who, early in their lives, considered full-time Christian ministry as a vocation. None of them felt compelled to pursue that interest, yet working part-time on the church staff gives a strong sense of satisfaction to those early vocational interests.

One of the big questions in all sizes of congregations has to do with determining which areas of ministry need staffing. Usually there are several areas that could use a staff person. The use of part-time people can meet more critical needs for ministry supervision than one full-time person.

The part-time staff member concept seems to have even greater implications for the small church. Every staff position at Frazer began as a part-time position. Most small churches cannot afford an additional full-time staff person, but can afford one or two part-time persons. Usually, two or three part-time people, doing specialized ministry, can accomplish much more than one full-time person.

This discussion of the use of part-time people should not be interpreted as a way to avoid paying people adequately, or to avoid paying benefits that normally come to full-time personnel. Part-time people should be paid well and benefits provided where needed. The goal of part-time staff is not to "hire cheap labor," but to maximize ministry effectiveness.

Many people inquire as to how part-time staff people can be trained. The best training for any staff person, part-time or full-time, is to visit a congregation that has an effective ministry in the particular area of that staff person's responsibility. People learn by experiencing and seeing. We simply pick out a couple of congregations that are doing what we feel needs to be done in an area of ministry, and let the staff person visit. Onsite training by a local church that is effectively doing the ministry is the best form of training.

Long-Term Tenure for Staff

I believe very strongly that staff people should be committed to long-term service on a church staff. The average tenure of staff persons in congregations is a little less than two years. I do not believe that very much constructive planning and implementation can take place in that narrow time frame of service on a church staff.

Every staff person who joins the staff at Frazer is asked to consider serving at least ten years. This does not mean the person has to stay ten years. But the person must join the staff with the intent of building a solid ministry in that specific area and following through with implementing that ministry. This long-term commitment is true for both part-time and full-time staff persons. All studies show there is a direct correlation between long-term commitments to ministry and the growth that takes place through those ministries.

Where to Look for Additional Staff

The best place to look for additional staff is within the life of the local congregation. Many churches always look outside to some other congregation as the best pool for future staff persons. I believe that the local church has a tremendous resource of potential part-time and full-time staff persons.

One of the advantages of looking for staff persons within the congregation is that the staff person is already accepted and appreciated by the congregation. If a staff person comes from the outside, it takes at least a year for the congregation to accept and trust this new leadership in ministry. If the staff person only stays two years, he/she will spend the last two or three months preparing for the move to the new responsibility, which means you only have about six or seven months of effective ministry! People who come from the local congregation start to work immediately because they are already accepted.

Another advantage of indigenous staff people is that you know these persons and have been exposed to their concepts of ministry. Every part-time staff person should come from the pool of volunteers who are already serving in that specific area of ministry. This means that a part-time or full-time staff person would already have been serving in that area of ministry, so you already know something about his/her effectiveness and expertise with that ministry and with relational skills. Hiring people on the church staff out of the local congregation should be a lot more reliable than hiring a stranger based on a résumé and an interview.

An example of this is a recent staff replacement at Frazer. A church member who was retiring from the Air Force had been extremely active in the work area on evangelism. He also was considering a church-related vocation following his retirement. We asked him to assume responsibility as minister of evangelism. He accepted and went to work the first day he came to the office. The church already loved and appreciated him, and he already had a grasp for the overall mission emphasis of the church, understood its priorities, and was already working with the volunteers in the area of evangelism.

Caution should be registered at this point. A person should not be hired too quickly, especially if you have doubts as to whether or not that person will work out. It could become a very difficult problem if someone in the church family were hired part-time and didn't function effectively. People always ask, "What do you do when you hire someone from the church family who does not work out?" My reply is simply, "You shouldn't have hired that person in the first place!" You should first have a solid grasp of that person's relational and technical skills through his or her involvement as a volunteer in ministry.

What to Look for in Potential Staff Persons

Some of the essential "ingredients" for future staff persons are Christian commitment, relational skills, and expertise. The most important of these is Christian commitment, and next would be relational skills.

Christian commitment is essential. If a person does not have a heart for ministry, and feel a calling to be part of a staff ministry, then that person will become a problem with staff members and with church members.

Some people have excellent technical expertise but poor relational skills. I would always favor the person with good relational skills over the person with good technical skills. People can learn technical skills far better than they can learn relational skills. On a church staff, a person who has poor relational skills will cause a lot of anguish for other staff members and will require a lot of time for other staff members to cover up some of the hard feelings and broken and damaged relationships caused by that staff person. A senior pastor doesn't need to spend his or her time "putting out fires."

Organizational Structure

Every church staff needs a well-defined organizational structure. Everybody needs to know the lines of accountability. This is true whether we are talking about large multiple staff congregations like Frazer, or about a small congregation with mostly volunteer staff. At Frazer we use what we refer to as a "Ministry and Personnel Chart."

This chart includes the names of every employee, every committee in the life of the congregation, and the lines of accountability for both ministry and personnel matters. Any lay person can look at the ministry and personnel chart and know exactly to whom any concern or question should be addressed. Each staff person knows to whom he or she is accountable. The Staff–Parish Committee uses this chart as a basic tool for understanding staff relationships.

I believe very strongly in giving people a lot of freedom. If a staff person has to be carefully supervised and watched, then that staff person should never have been hired. I believe in a very flexible job description. I believe in a job description that leaves open wide parameters for utilizing the special gifts and talents that each staff member brings to the job.

This principle is well illustrated in the experience of Rudy Heintzelman, a diaconal minister who is responsible for ministries and programs at Frazer. Rudy has been on the Frazer staff for the past seven years. He often shares the job description that he claims I gave him when he came. He says I told him the following three things:

1. If I know everything that is going on in this congregation, there is not enough going on. Keep me informed on major issues.
2. Never let me catch you doing anything a volunteer could or should be doing. Your job is not to do ministry but rather to train laity to do ministry.
3. If I thought I could be doing a program better than you, neither of us would be necessary.

I basically tell the people that I supervise, and encourage them to tell the people they supervise, that they will have tremendous freedom to exercise their leadership and ministry, but with accountability to the person supervising them. If you can't give broad latitude to a staff member, you either hired the wrong person or didn't need a person in that position!

How to Build Team Spirit

A strong team spirit is essential in developing and building a staff. I often say to the staff that we are to model the church for the whole congregation. The kind of encouragement, support, and love we exhibit is the kind of model we would like to place before the congregation as a whole.

Our church staff meets every Wednesday morning at 8:30. The eleven members of the senior staff meet for thirty minutes to look at any programming or administrative needs. The entire staff meets at 9:00. We begin with a devotional that is led each week by a different staff person. We then share concerns that are either personal or from our specific ministries, and then we pray about these. Prayer partners are selected so that each staff member has two staff persons praying for him or her each week.

The church staff takes a break for coffee every morning at 10:00 in an informal setting. This is important because it is not structured and gives people an opportunity to relate to each other and share personal and family concerns as well as dreams for ministry. We use Monday morning at 10:00 for a time of specific prayer for staff concerns.

The entire church staff eats together once a month. The congregation pays for this. The staff member who has a birthday that month selects the restaurant. It is a time for fellowship and for building relationships.

The sense of togetherness is extremely important in a church staff. It takes time to build team spirit, but it is essential when critical situations arise, such as when two staff people have reserved the same room for the same event, or two staff people have reserved the bus at the same time. I can honestly say that the spirit of the staff at Frazer is not to fight aggressively for the room or the bus, but rather to look at the other staff person's needs and responsibilities first. Frazer staff people in such situations wind up trying to be more helpful to the other staff person than to themselves! This is a real witness to the model of what the church can be.

Community Involvement

I also encourage staff people to become involved in the community. One member of the Frazer staff is president of the largest civic club in town. Three of us serve as chaplains for athletic teams in different high schools. And one staff person serves as a chaplain to a sports program at Auburn University at Montgomery.

People on the youth staff volunteer to take up lunch money in the junior high schools. This is a tremendous help to school systems looking for volunteers. The youth staff simply wear a tee shirt indicating they are from Frazer and, as a result, they meet unchurched kids and establish relationships to which the young people can refer later. Staff members should not spend all their time behind desks in the church building. They should be out in the community witnessing through their natural webs of social contacts. The same thing goes for lay volunteers who carry out and represent the ministries of small congregations.

Another area of staff involvement is with inactive members. We periodically give staff members the names of persons who have become inactive. We ask the staff to visit inactives because it is good for staff people and inactives to interact. In as many ways as possible, staff members need to see "the big picture" of what is happening in the congregation. They cannot afford to become insulated in their own office or in their own specific ministry.

Priorities of the Senior Pastor

The most important functions of the senior pastor are to give leadership to the congregation, to lead worship, and to focus on selecting lay leadership and staff persons. The pastor needs to be a leader who helps to see the vision for the congregation, and then gives leadership in moving toward that vision.

Worship is the one event that is attended by more people than any other single event. The senior pastor must have responsibility for making the worship service indigenous, exciting, and alive.

The senior pastor also needs to be effective in selecting lay people and staff. My concept of a pastor is something like that of a coach. If a coach places the quarterback at tackle, and the tackle at quarterback, the coach is in for a long season. If the senior pastor, through the Nominating Committee, makes bad choices for lay leadership, the church will be greatly handicapped. If the senior pastor does not build an effective staff, then the senior pastor's work is greatly extended and the effective work of the congregation is diminished.

In all of these ways, the senior pastor's task is to understand the total working model of the growing congregation and to strengthen the model at every point—especially in the encouragement and empowerment of a creative staff.

CHAPTER 11
DEPEND ON GOD

After examining each of the other ten steps, we come at last to the most important part of the model for growth: *To depend ultimately on God.* The most talented people designing the best programs will never be a substitute for the fact that this is God's church and God's hand of blessing is required for the church to succeed.

In His Steps

For this reason, at Frazer, our theme is "In His Steps." The task of the church is to discover God's will for the church in Christ, and then to move forward in his will. We encourage people who are confronted with questions and decisions to ask the question, "What would Jesus do in this situation?" Christian maturity comes as our decisions become synonymous with God's dream for us and for our congregation.

A beautiful description of the early church is found in Acts 2:42-47. This passage describes how the people prayed, studied, had fellowship, reached out to others, were unified, and witnessed boldly to their faith. Verse 47 says, "And day by day the Lord added to their number those who were being saved." God gave the results. The ultimate growth of the church comes from the initiative of God, blessing the efforts of the people.

The task of the church is to do the best job possible in prayerful planning, and then to put the plan into practice. We must be constantly reminded of Paul's instruction for the Church at Corinth in 1 Corinthians 3:6 when he said, "I planted, Apollos watered, but God gave the growth." Our ultimate dependence is on God.

Many times in my ministry I thought I had a great idea and I worked hard to make something happen. I did everything except depend on

God. I found that my ideas were not so brilliant; the program did not work; and nothing was done to help bring about God's kingdom.

God created the church and invited us to be a part of it. We did not create the church, so we do not have the innate ability to determine what the church should do and be. The church is God's church and God must give direction to its ministry.

God's Plan

A key passage for me is the seventh chapter of Judges. Gideon was about to go into battle with the Midianites. Gideon was feeling very comfortable about the battle, but God gave him a warning in verse two: ". . . The troops with you are too many for me to give the Midianites into their hand. Israel would only take the credit away from me, saying, 'My own hand has delivered me.'" God wanted to give Israel the victory, but did not want the people to assume that they had accomplished this on their own. God's answer to this situation is to reduce the size of Gideon's army, telling all the people who are afraid to return and depart from Mt. Gilead. Twenty-two thousand people left, and only 10,000 remained.

This was somewhat threatening to Gideon because he wanted to be sure his army was strong enough. He was very perplexed. Then God told him there were still too many people and he needed to reduce the army further. God used a strange means of determining who should fight. He told Gideon to bring the people to the water and tell them that they should drink the water. The manner in which they drank the water would determine whether Gideon could use them to fight or not. Gideon brought the people to the water. The Lord said to him (verse 5), "All those who lap the water with their tongues, as a dog laps, you shall put to one side; all those who kneel down to drink, putting their hands to their mouths, you shall put to the other side." The amazing thing is that the number who lapped the water from their hand to their mouth was only 300. The rest of the people knelt to drink the water.

Naturally, Gideon wanted to keep the people who knelt to drink, but was shocked when God ordered him to take the 300 instead. God told him to send the rest of the people home. Gideon knew the very basic principle of dependence upon God. He took the 300 men into battle and experienced a marvelous triumph.

The whole point of this account is that God wanted to show Gideon that God was the one responsible for Israel's victory, not Israel's military might and genius. That is precisely the same lesson God is teaching the church today. God expects us to be as well prepared as possible, but we cannot be involved in meaningful ministry based on our own talents and gifts. God created the church and called it into being, and God knows what is best for it. Even though God's plan often seems ridiculous to us, biblical history and personal experience have proven that God's plan always works!

The most important ingredient in helping your church grow is ultimate dependence on God. Whenever a congregation recognizes its own weakness and trusts in God as its strength, that will become a strong congregation in effective ministry!

I believe the church today is sitting on the edge of one of the most incredible opportunities for ministry. I believe we have at our fingertips everything necessary for the church to be a vital force in today's world. What God is looking for is people who will plan and prepare, then trust and depend upon God's guidance.

History or His-Story

In a real sense I have a feeling that the history of Frazer is His-Story. It has been a tremendous joy to witness the meaningful ministries and growth of Frazer. But, I am more excited about the future because of the vision God has placed in the hearts of the Frazer family and the desire of lay people to depend upon God and devote themselves to being involved in God's ministry.

Recently I was walking down the hall on a Sunday morning and stopped by a children's Sunday school class. They had a little plastic church building that they used to collect their offering. I was fascinated by the toy and picked it up to look at it. Very quickly one of the little boys said, "Be careful, John Ed, you have our church in your hands." That statement both inspired and intimidated me. In a larger sense, God has entrusted the church into our hands. What an awesome opportunity!

I love the passage in Acts 4 where the early church was so involved in meeting the needs of the community around them. Acts 4:34 says, "There was not a needy person among them. . . ." The experience of the early church was described in this way: "Awe came upon everyone, because many wonders and signs were being done by the apostles"

(Acts 2:43). Everyone kept feeling a sense of awe and many signs and wonders were taking place through the apostles. This tremendous witness caused people to respond to the grace of God to the point that ". . . day by day the Lord added to their number those who were being saved" (Acts 2:47).

Shake This Place

This kind of ministry was further described in Acts 4:31: "When they had prayed, the place in which they were gathered together was shaken. . . ." I pray that God will so lead the church in the last decade of this century to become so involved in proclaiming the "good news" of Jesus Christ, and ministering to people in need, that people in the future will experience the Christian church as a place of signs and wonders and awe! My prayer is that God would "shake this place"!

And God will, when we depend on Him!

APPENDIX
SAMPLE JOEL COMMITTEE REPORTS

FRAZER MEMORIAL UNITED METHODIST CHURCH
JOEL COMMITTEE REPORT
May 15, 1980

Bill Baldwin	Greg McKinnon
Bill Clark	Butch McPherson
George Clark	Stan Magner
Archie Coleman	John Ed Mathison
Robert Duke	Pat Morgan
Dave Elyea	Walter Nanney
Ed Emfinger	Mike Penick
Jerry Fulmer	Johnny Redding
Andy Harris	Jack Thompson
Charles Holston	Chester Williams
Bill Hoekenga	Frank Wright
Mary Jane Lyerly	Mike Hutson
Loette Lee	Benny Nolen

This committee studied extensively the past history of Frazer and prayerfully projected some growth figures for the future. Based on this study, this report is presented to the Administrative Board for approval and action.

LONG-RANGE PLANNING PROPOSAL

Year	Sunday School (Estimated)	Worship Attendance (Estimated)
1976	380	718
1977	472	887

Year	Sunday School (Estimated)	Worship Attendance (Estimated)
1978	533	1,040
1979	651	1,193
1980	800	1,400
1981	950	1,600
1982	1,100	1,800
1983	1,300	2,000
1984	1,400	2,200
1985	1,500	2,450
1986	1,700	2,650
1987	1,800	2,900
1988	1,900	3,100
1989	2,000	3,300
1990	2,100	3,500

The above figures show that in 1982 we will be accommodating all the people that our present facilities can handle. By 1982, additional worship space and Sunday School space must be provided. In order to have this provided by 1982, a decision of what to build and where to build it should be reached by the end of 1980.

A. *FACILITIES*

1. We suggest that the Building Committee meet with the building consultant to discuss the feasibility of how much worship space and Sunday School space could be provided on our present property (with special attention given to parking and access to the Atlanta Highway). The committee would also discuss the possibility of utilizing the present Sanctuary and Fellowship Hall for some other function.

2. We suggest that we investigate the possibility of selling the current facilities consisting of buildings and five acres nearby to build a new church plant. This is pursued because (a) we will need more parking and access avenues to the main arteries of traffic to accommodate the projected people and (b) it might be better stewardship to plan and build what we need rather than

trying to renovate two buildings (present Fellowship Hall and Sanctuary) to use them for functions other than those for which they were originally built.

B. *STAFF*

1. Develop staff needs on an annual basis with positions based on available personnel. Basically a staff member should be added with every 350 new members.

C. *MINISTRIES*

1. Suggest portable classrooms for Sunday School to meet immediate needs and buy as needed.
2. The key to the continued growth of Frazer is the assimilation of new members—programming and staff must address this.
3. Teacher training program for prospective teachers to train them before they are needed in the classrooms.
4. Devise ways of increasing participation at the 8:40 a.m. hour both in Sunday School and Worship.
5. Move with reasonable haste toward a television ministry.
6. Explore the possibility of the use of a computer to assist in ministry.
7. Pursue recreation facilities.

JOEL COMMITTEE REPORT
1986

The Joel Committee was charged with the responsibility of "dreaming God's dream for Frazer" and making long range plans for Frazer. The Joel Committee has met numerous times in recent weeks and gathered a large bank of data as basis for this report. Listed below are the members of the Joel Committee:

Mike Hutson, Lay Leader	Lynn Gowan, Sunday School
Terry Taylor, Adm. Bd.	Marie Parma, Music
Jerry Kemp, Finance	Cheryl Rayford, I Singles
Sam Windham, Stewardship	Byron Mills, PTS
Paul Sims, COM	David Higginbotham, Youth
Terry Owens, Trustees	Jack Fowler, Evangelism
Jim Dickins, Education	Betty Henry, Children
Larry Robinson, Bldg.	Angie Morrow, Nursery
Committee	Don Stansel
Bill Clark	Bill Hoekenga
Chester Williams	Rusty Salter
Jean Williams	Rush Stallings
Louise Hollis	Bob Corwin
Robert G. Lee	

Listed below are the averages and projections for Sunday school and worship. The Committee has a computerized study showing the average attendance for worship each month and the average attendance for each Sunday school department each month for the past five years and the projections for each month through 1991 based on the growth rate of the past five years.

Year	Average Sunday School Attendance	Average Worship Attendance
1976	380	718
1977	472	887
1978	533	1,116
1979	651	1,173
1980	810	1,501
1981	878	1,701

Year	Average Sunday School Attendance	Average Worship Attendance
1982	989	1,951
1983	1,154	2,133
1984	1,342	2,402
1985	1,528	2,710
	Projected	
1986	1,700	2,900
1987	1,900	3,100
1988	2,100	3,300
1989	2,300	3,600
1990	2,500	3,800
1991	2,600	4,000
1992	2,800	4,300
1993	3,000	4,500

The Joel Committee perceives that our growth will be affected in the future by our ability to provide facilities, staff, and programs (ministries). Each of the three is an essential part of the triangle.

FACILITIES

1. The first priority for facilities is to provide additional nursery space. It is suggested that the rooms on the south side of the hall, (81-86) across from the present nursery, be converted.
2. The next priority is worship space. With the opening of the new lobby area and the removal of the partition to the back wall, additional space will be available. We propose that a committee consisting of Bob Kline, Church Administrator; Terry Owens, Board of Trustees; Larry Robinson, Chairman of Building Committee; Chester Williams, Contractor; Rush Stallings, Parking Usher; Terry Taylor, Administrative Board Chairman; and Don Stansell, Architect; be commissioned to study the feasibility of enlarging the present sanctuary. The report should include the maximum seats that could be gained through renovation, and the approximate cost be included in the report which is to be made by July 1, 1987. Based on this report consideration for future worship facilities will be made. Music expansion is a part of the worship facility.

3. The next priority is for additional office space. We suggest that a two-story building be constructed in the courtyard area nearest the present offices. This would keep all offices in close proximity and future expansion could use the rooms on the south side of the hall across from the present offices.

4. The next priority would be for additional rooms for the children's ministry. The first suggestion is to add a second floor to the present fellowship hall and devote the upstairs to children's ministry. It is suggested that these first four priorities be listed as "New Building Needs," to which people may pledge in the 1986 In His Steps Campaign.

5. Parking is the next priority. Utilization of parking in Astraddle Square and utilization of Park and Ride will determine the urgency of this need.

STAFF

We suggest that the Staff/Parish Committee continue its policy of hiring a staff person for every 200-300 new members. We affirm the concept of part-time staff and the utilization of persons from the congregation.

PROGRAM (MINISTRIES)

1. We affirm the on-going ministries of the church and suggest that each program be evaluated on the basis of (1) whether or not it meets a need, (2) whether or not it is a vehicle for making disciples. The present programs and ministries are affirmed and we challenge the Council on Ministries and the Frazer family to become involved in new areas of ministry where there are perceived needs and opportunities for making disciples.

2. We strongly affirm the television ministry and strongly endorse its expansion where opportunities present themselves.

3. We encourage the expansion of the In Christ Way Ministry and affirm the debt retirement emphasis.

4. We encourage the congregation to become more deeply involved in the counseling ministry and to look for opportunities to establish a counseling center at Frazer. It is hoped that this will also expand to some specialized treatment in alcohol and drug abuse.

5. We suggest that the Joel Committee should meet again within two years.

FOR FURTHER READING

The following titles are available from Discipleship Resources, P.O. Box 189, Nashville, TN 37202, (615) 340-7284.

Suzanne G. Braden and Shirley F. Clement, *Caring Evangelism: A Visitation Program for Congregations,* Leader's Guide and Participant's Workbook. Order Nos. DR111 and EV178.

W. James Cowell, *Extending Your Congregation's Welcome: Internal Climate and Intentional Outreach.* Order No. DR068.

W. James Cowell, *Incorporating New Members: Bonds of Believing, Belonging, and Becoming.* Order No. DR112.

Roger Deschner, *Singing in the Church Choir.* Order No. W156K.

H. Eddie Fox and George Morris, *Faith-Sharing: Dynamic Christian Witnessing by Invitation.* Order No. DR039.

Joe Harding and Ralph Mohney, *Vision 2000: Planning for Ministry into the Next Century.* Order No. DR098.

Thomas R. Hawkins, *Building God's People: A Workbook for Empowering Servant Leaders.* Order No. LA070.

John Ed Mathison, *Every Member in Ministry: Involving Laity and Inactives.* Order No. EV162.

Herb Mather, *Gifts Discovery Workshop: Leader's Guide.* Order No. ST046; and *Gifts Discovery Workshop: My Giftbook.* Order No. ST045. This is a very concise and helpful exploration of basic spiritual gifts.

Craig Miller, *Baby Boomer Spirituality: Ten Essential Values of a Generation.* Order No. DR106.

Craig Miller, *Encounters with Jesus: A Group Study in Baby Boomer Spirituality.* Order No. DR113.

Time and Talent Inventory. A brochure for registering your congregation's ministry goals. Order No. E244T.

David Watson, *Covenant Discipleship: Christian Formation Through Mutual Accountability.* Order No. DR091.

David A. Wiltse, *Designing the Worship Bulletin.* Order No. W160K.

NOTES

NOTES

NOTES

NOTES